Tom Brady

FOOTBALL ⬤ SUPERSTARS

Tiki Barber

Tom Brady

John Elway

Brett Favre

Peyton Manning

Dan Marino

Donovan McNabb

Joe Montana

Walter Payton

Jerry Rice

Ben Roethlisberger

Barry Sanders

FOOTBALL ● SUPERSTARS

Tom Brady

Rachel A. Koestler-Grack

Checkmark Books™

An imprint of Facts On File, Inc.

TOM BRADY

Checkmark Books
An imprint of Infobase Publishing
132 West 31st Street
New York NY 10001

Library of Congress Cataloging-in-Publication Data
Koestler-Grack, Rachel A., 1973-
  Tom Brady / Rachel A. Koestler-Grack.
    p. cm. — (Football superstars)
  Includes bibliographical references and index.
  ISBN 978-0-7910-9689-5 (hardcover)
  ISBN 978-1-60413-320-2 (paperback)
  1. Brady, Tom, 1977- 2. Football players—United States—Biography—Juvenile literature.
3. Quarterbacks (Football)—United States—Biography—Juvenile literature. I. Title.
II. Series.

  GV939.B685K64 2008
  796.332092—dc22
  [B]
                    2007040953

Checkmark Books are available at special discounts when purchased in bulk quantities for businesses, associations, institutions, or sales promotions. Please call our Special Sales Department in New York at (212) 967-8800 or (800) 322-8755.

You can find Chelsea House on the World Wide Web at http://www.chelseahouse.com

Text design by Erik Lindstrom
Cover design by Ben Peterson

Printed in the United States of America

Bang EJB 10 9 8 7 6 5 4 3 2 1

This book is printed on acid-free paper.

All links and Web addresses were checked and verified to be correct at the time of publication. Because of the dynamic nature of the Web, some addresses and links may have changed since publication and may no longer be valid.

CONTENTS

Super Bowl Upset

They were known as the "Greatest Show on Turf." Thanks to a dynamic passing attack, the St. Louis Rams' offense scored more than 500 total points per season from 1999 to 2001. Led by **quarterback** and two-time **National Football League (NFL)** MVP Kurt Warner and three-time Associated Press Offensive Player of the Year **running back** Marshall Faulk, the Rams won Super Bowl XXXIV, in 2000, and were overwhelming favorites to win another title in 2002. Faulk was one of the NFL's greatest two-way threats, becoming only the second player in league history to top the 1,000-**yard** mark in both rushing and receiving in a season. He also set a new NFL record for most **touchdowns** in a season with 26. Certainly, the New England Patriots, with rookie quarterback Tom Brady, would be no match for the Rams in Super Bowl XXXVI.

SUPER BOWL GLORY

Brady had a remarkable year with the Patriots. Climbing from fourth-string on the **depth chart**, Brady had beat out **veteran** Damon Huard as the Patriots' **backup** quarterback during the 2001 training camp. In the second game of the season, against the New York Jets, New England's starting quarterback, Drew Bledsoe, was sidelined with an injury. Although Brady was in his second year with the team, he was essentially a rookie when he entered the game against the Jets. After the Patriots lost their first two games, Brady led them to wins in 11 of their last 14 games to help the team finish 11–5 during the regular season. Surprising football fans everywhere, the **American Football Conference (AFC)** East Division champion Patriots muscled through the playoffs and stood at the threshold of winning Super Bowl XXXVI. However, to many fans and experts alike, the night of February 3, 2002, was supposed to mark the end of the Patriots' fairy-tale run through the playoffs.

Despite being two-touchdown underdogs, the Patriots jumped out to a commanding 17-3 lead with less than two minutes left in the third quarter. But the Rams were about to fight back. They drove all the way to the Patriots' 3-yard line with about 11 minutes left to play in the game. On fourth-and-goal, the Rams decided to go for a touchdown with a quarterback sneak. However, Kurt Warner **fumbled** on the play, and the ball was picked up by Patriots **safety** Tebucky Jones, who returned the ball 97 yards for an apparent touchdown. The score would have increased the Patriots' lead to 24-3, but a **holding** penalty on New England linebacker Willie McGinest erased the touchdown. Instead, the Rams got a **first down** at the New England 1-yard line. Two plays later, St. Louis scored a touchdown on a Warner run to cut the deficit to 17-10 with 9:33 left. The Rams then held the Patriots scoreless on their next two possessions to set up a thrilling finish. With just 1:51 left in the game, the Rams took over with a chance to tie the game. Warner then worked his magic: In just three pass plays, he drove the Rams

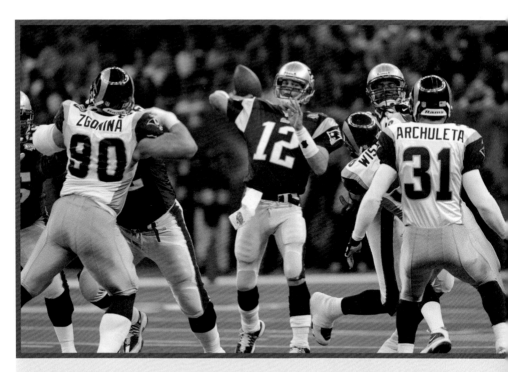

New England Patriots quarterback Tom Brady throws a pass during the third quarter of Super Bowl XXXVI at the Louisiana Superdome, on February 3, 2002. Brady was named MVP of the game after completing 16 of 27 passes for 145 yards and a touchdown in the Patriots' 20-17 win over the St. Louis Rams.

55 yards, capping the **drive** with a 26-yard touchdown pass to **wide receiver** Ricky Proehl that tied the game at 17-17 with 1:30 left to play.

The game would come down to one final drive. With no time-outs left, New England took possession of the ball at its own 17-yard line. In six plays, Brady managed to move the ball all the way to the Rams' 31-yard line, where he spiked the ball with just seven seconds left in the game. Patriots kicker Adam Vinatieri then took the field to attempt a 48-yard **field goal**. He calmly kicked the ball through the uprights, and the Patriots became the first team in NFL history to win the Super Bowl on the last play of the game.

The Patriots had pulled off one of the biggest upsets in Super Bowl history, defeating St. Louis by a score of 20-17. Facing off against the NFL's Most Valuable Player and Offensive

TOM BRADY'S SUPER BOWL ITUNES PLAYLIST

Like most young people, Tom Brady keeps his iPod within reach, especially before a big game. Here is a list of the songs Brady listened to in the locker room before Super Bowl XXXIX. The list reveals Brady's eclectic taste in music; although his favorite group is U2, which has three songs on his playlist.

1. "Dream On" by Aerosmith
2. "Lose Yourself" by Eminem
3. "Possum Kingdom" by The Toadies
4. "If I Can't" by 50 Cent
5. "Fell on Black Days" by Soundgarden
6. "Bittersweet Symphony" by The Verve
7. "Award Tour" by A Tribe Called Quest
8. "Mysterious Ways" by U2
9. "I Can" by Nas
10. "Shiver" by Coldplay
11. "My Name Is" by Eminem
12. "I Still Haven't Found What I'm Looking For" by U2
13. "Jesus Walks" by Kanye West
14. "Beast of Burden" by the Rolling Stones
15. "Wonderwall" by Oasis
16. "Black" by Pearl Jam
17. "Sunday Bloody Sunday" by U2
18. "Encore" by Jay-Z

(Source: *Greatness: The Rise of Tom Brady* by *The Boston Globe*)

Player of the Year did not faze Brady. He convinced himself it was just another game. At 24 years and 185 days old, he became the youngest quarterback to win the Super Bowl. And so began the New England Patriots' dynasty, which would include three Super Bowl victories in four years.

Practically overnight, Brady had become a celebrity. He suddenly was the poster child for the NFL. Humble and charming, he wooed the media and fans throughout the world. He became America's sweetheart, representing the principles this country was built on—hard work, honesty, and dedication. A two-time Super Bowl MVP, as well as 2004 *Sports Illustrated* Player of the Year and 2005 Sportsman of the Year, Brady has come a long way in his seven years as a starting NFL quarterback. "When you are a kid, everyone wants to grow up and play sports," Brady said in *Greatness: The Rise of Tom Brady*. Still, there are times when he is sitting around with his mom and dad and suddenly turns to them and says, "Can you believe this?"

Huggers and Kissers

The Bradys are not afraid to show affection. They are a family of huggers and kissers. In fact, after a Patriots game, it may be surprising to see quarterback Tom Brady, win or lose, greeting old friends with a kiss on the cheek. But it all seems normal to anyone who knows the Brady family. The roots of their friendliness can be traced back to a Catholic schoolboy in San Francisco—Thomas Brady (Sr.). His Irish father, Harry, had trouble expressing his emotions. Thomas vowed never to close himself up that way. Instead, he wanted to raise his children to be open, loving, and giving to the world.

When he grew older, Thomas attended the University of San Francisco, and during his final semester, in 1968, he joined the Marines. He was set to go to Vietnam right after he graduated from college. In May of that year, however, Thomas tore cartilage in his knee while working out. He was discharged from the Marines as a lance corporal. So, he shifted gears and took a job selling insurance.

MEETING GALYNN

One day in 1968, Thomas knocked on the apartment door of a flight attendant named Galynn Johnson. She did not buy any insurance. In fact, they never even talked about it. Instead, they fell into a long conversation about their families. Galynn had been born in Browerville, Minnesota, a small town about 140 miles northwest of Minneapolis. She was the daughter of the town barber who also dreamed of becoming a farmer. Gordon Johnson did not like the hustle and bustle of downtown Browerville. Little by little, at 50¢ a haircut, he saved up enough money to buy his dream—a farm three miles outside of town. The family moved to their country home when Galynn was a sophomore in high school.

Galynn had an uncle and aunt who lived in Santa Ana, California. From time to time, they visited Minnesota, bringing with them wonderful tales of lemon trees and orange groves. The stories enticed Galynn into making a dramatic decision. One afternoon, while working at an advertising agency in Minneapolis, she read an advertisement in the paper for a stewardess program at Trans World Airlines. A month later, she was attending classes at the training school in St. Louis. Galynn chose to work on domestic flight routes. That way, she could live in San Francisco. (TWA's international crews were based in New York City.)

Once Tom met Galynn, it did not take him long to realize they were meant for each other. He asked her to go out on a date the following Friday. It was a whirlwind courtship. Six months after that knock on the door, Tom and Galynn were standing at the wedding altar. After they got married, they moved to San Mateo, a suburb south of San Francisco.

The town is bisected by an old highway that has run through California since the days when the region belonged to Spain. The road is called Alameda de las Pulgas, or the "Avenue of the Fleas." Throughout the alameda, the neighborhoods are layered on a series of ladderlike plateaus. The Bradys lived on Portola Drive, where they raised four children. Three daughters came first—Maureen, Julie, and Nancy. Then, on August 3, 1977, Tommy was born.

SPORTS FANATICS

Finally, after his wife had three girls, Tom Sr. was glad to have another male in the house. But living in a family of four girls and two boys, Tom Sr. and Tommy still felt outnumbered at times. As soon as Tommy turned five, Tom Sr. began taking him to the California Golf Club—a private men's only club in nearby San Francisco. Here, father and son could have a little no-girls-allowed time. On Sunday mornings, they would arrive at the golf course by six thirty and be back home in time to go to church at 11:00 A.M. By age 10, Tommy was quite the young golfer. He was perfectly comfortable around the older men, carrying on conversations and joking with them. Although friendly and outgoing like his father, at times, Tommy still carried a hint of Galynn's reservedness. Even at a young age, Tommy's competitive nature was already becoming apparent. It showed in his wild temper, especially while playing video games. After losing a game, he would often throw the controller across the room. (There is still a hole in one of the Bradys' walls as proof of one of his fits.)

All of the Bradys were sports fanatics. Immediately after attending Mass during football season, they piled in the family car and headed off to tailgate at Candlestick Park before San Francisco 49ers games. It did not take long for Tommy to become a loyal fan of 49ers quarterback Joe Montana. Later at home, the family would even watch a replay of that day's game. Tommy never got bored of watching the games again on film.

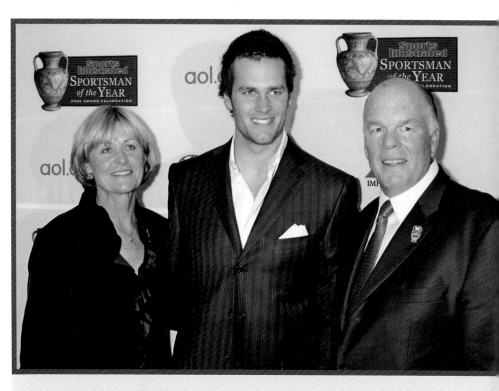

Tom Brady comes from a close-knit family, all of whom enjoyed both playing and watching sports. The youngest of four children, Brady is pictured here with his mother, Galynn, and his father, Tom Sr., in December 2005 at the *Sports Illustrated* Sportsman of the Year banquet in New York City.

He was enthralled by Montana's gift of making big plays at the most crucial times. In addition to watching games, the Bradys also enjoyed playing sports. Galynn was an excellent tennis player, and, like both Toms, she enjoyed playing golf. Tom Sr. also was a rough and tumble basketball player, who did not believe in calling fouls when he played pickup games. The girls all played soccer and softball. In high school, Maureen became a star pitcher, with 14 perfect games. She eventually earned a scholarship to Fresno State University. Nancy was not only a great athlete, but she also was a respected member of the debate team at Hillsdale High School. She practiced on her parents and even convinced Tom Sr. to change his mind about several subjects. Tom played baseball and, of course, football.

Due to the fact that the children were so busy participating in sports and other extracurricular activities, the Bradys found it necessary to use a kitchen calendar to keep track of all the children's athletic games. The year Tommy was in eighth grade, 315 games were scribbled throughout the calendar squares. Even if both parents could not attend a game, at least one of them was always there.

Tom Brady (Sr.) coached the basketball teams at St. Gregory's—the parochial grade school his son attended. He insisted everyone on the team play in each game, which angered some of the parents. Tommy was one of the basketball team's star players, but he was a better baseball player. He showed real ability as a catcher. For some reason, however, baseball did not excite him, either. He thought the sport showcased individual talents too much. Growing up, Tommy had always worked together with his sisters and parents. He understood the value of teamwork. He liked the camaraderie of football. "If you choose to alienate yourself or put yourself apart," he later said in *Moving the Chains: Tom Brady and the Pursuit of Everything*, "play tennis. Play golf."

AN INTRODUCTION TO A NEW SPORT

Tom continued to play sports at Junípero Serra High School, named after the Franciscan priest who brought the Catholic religion to California. This male-only college preparatory school was made up of low, sprawling buildings that hugged a central courtyard. In the yard, a statue of the Madonna was surrounded by rows of picnic tables. Serra was primarily known as a baseball school. Jim Fregosi, a shortstop with Major League Baseball's California Angels, who later managed several MLB teams, graduated from the school in 1959. When he was younger, Tom had watched a Serra Padres team led by future MLB star Barry Bonds. The high school's sole claim to football fame was Lynn Swann, who after graduating went on to the University of Southern California and a Hall of Fame career at wide receiver with the Pittsburgh Steelers. However, as far as the coaches at Serra were concerned, they simply thought that Tom would be their next great catcher.

Tom excelled in baseball, but no one expected him to play football at Serra. However, the pull to play football was pretty strong, even though the game did not come to him as easily as baseball did. Between Tom's freshman and sophomore years, Serra's starting junior-varsity quarterback left the team, which opened up an opportunity for Tom. That spring and summer, he and his father went to quarterback camps in Arizona and at the University of California, Berkeley. Tom Sr. also decided they should talk with a passing expert named Tom Martinez, who was the head coach at the College of San Mateo, where he also ran a quarterback camp.

Martinez was a rare sports specialist who had developed a system for teaching a specific skill extraordinarily well. Each sport has its own set of experts who get paid to help young athletes develop their skills. Martinez decided to dedicate himself to the art of throwing a football. He broke down the mechanics of throwing a forward pass—from the number of steps the quarterback takes to the position of his hand before he releases the ball. Along the way, he developed his own training techniques. Martinez worked with Tom on every aspect of what a quarterback should do. He explained how a quarterback should start his drop in the **pocket** with his dominant foot—the same foot as his throwing hand—forward. This move makes it easier to pivot and retreat. It also allows the quarterback to drop back faster, giving him more time to read the defense and throw the ball. Martinez described how 49ers head coach Bill Walsh had taught Montana and his other quarterbacks to take little, shuffling steps into the pocket. Martinez gave Tom the option of shuffling or standing still. He emphasized the benefit of a short, powerful stride when throwing a football. A wide stride, he argued, results in a short-armed throw.

During Tom's training, Martinez pointed out the difference between a C throw and a U throw. The names of these throws come from the position of the hand on the ball at the time of release. If a player holds the ball by its side when he throws, his hand forms a C shape. If he grips the ball underneath, his fingers make a U. The U throw is how most people throw a football, but this grip offers less control and causes a wobbly toss. While he practiced with Martinez, Tom took detailed notes, which he still refers to today. Tom appreciated the way Martinez could explain why certain passing techniques worked. The amount of personal attention was priceless as well. After working with Martinez, the would-be baseball player, who had never played football until ninth grade, was ready to make a change that would affect the rest of his life.

CHOOSING FOOTBALL

With the help of Martinez, Tom was leaning more and more toward focusing on football by the start of his junior year at Serra in 1993. He liked the way playing quarterback engaged his mind, forcing him to figure things out. This new way of thinking was something his teachers also noticed in the classroom. His curiosity to know the how and why of certain subjects led him to take classes such as geometry, architecture, and ethics.

Tom applied hard work and perseverance to everything he did. After he played junior varsity his sophomore year, Serra football coach Tom MacKenzie said he had "a Division 1 arm, but a Division 5 lower body." That comment was all it took to light a fire under Tom. In practice, MacKenzie pushed the players to do a footwork drill called the Five Dots. Most of the players loathed this tedious exercise. But Tom built a replica of the Five Dots in his backyard. He practiced the drill every morning before school to increase his lower body strength.

"I've never been real fleet of foot," Brady said years later in *Moving the Chains.* "I enjoyed the struggle of it. I gained a lot out of it, in terms of mental toughness."

Before too long, Tom's days fell into a pattern. During the off-season, he would rush home from school, do his homework, and then dart over to the Pacific Athletic Club in Redwood City for a three- to four-hour workout. Despite his hard work, Tom hardly set the world on fire during his two varsity years at Serra. The team went 6–4 the first season and 5–5 the next. In those 20 games, Tom completed 219 passes for 3,514 yards and 33 touchdowns. These numbers were modest compared to California's top quarterback in 1994—Kevin Feterik of Los Alamitos High School—who passed for more than 3,000 yards in his senior year alone. In fact, Tom only holds a couple of school records—completions (22) and atttempts (41) in a game and most attempts for a season (273). Most of the Serra passing records are shared by the Freitas brothers, Jesse (who played for the San Diego Chargers in the mid-1970s) and Jim.

There were some disappointments along the way, too. In Tom's junior year, Serra experienced devastating back-to-back defeats, 63-6 and 44-0. Also, during his senior season, Serra only needed to win its final two games to make the Central Coast Section playoffs. Tom completed just 13 of 41 passes for a meager 188 yards in those two games. Serra got beat 12-0 and 27-6. Right after his junior season in 1993, Coach MacKenzie called Tom into his office and told him that the coaching staff had decided not to nominate him for the all-league team. His statistics were good enough to be nominated, but the coaches knew he could do better. MacKenzie wanted to teach Tom that things in life are earned, not given. Even though it must have been a rough blow, Tom took it in stride. He accepted the challenge and worked harder. He truly believed in the motto: "It's not what people think you can do, it's what you do."

MacKenzie saw in Tom something coaches rarely find in young players. "He's confident, but not arrogant," MacKenzie

Nicknamed the Big House, Michigan Stadium is the largest on-campus stadium in the United States, with a capacity of more than 107,000. One of the primary reasons Tom Brady chose to play football at the University of Michigan was to have the opportunity to compete at a high level; something he would not get by attending a school that was closer to home.

said in *Greatness: The Rise of Tom Brady.* "He believes in him-self, but it's not cockiness. He didn't moan when I told him [about all-league]. That's been his history."

During the off-season, Tom attended summer camps and participated in a 7-on-7 passing tournament. He displayed his grasp of the basics to the college and professional scouts who were in attendance. How he performed for Serra was important, but scouts put more stock in the summer camps. The coaches at the prestigious football camp at the University of California, Berkeley, named Tom MVP. This honor ensured that college

MICHIGAN FOOTBALL

When a talented football player chooses a college, much thought goes into the decision-making process. The reputation of the school's football team is important, such as its winning record or its coaching staff. Playing at one of the traditional college football powers, such as the University of Michigan, often ensures that a player gets noticed by NFL teams. Any talented player who wants to be drafted by an NFL team will want to play football at one of those schools. Tom Brady chose Michigan because its football tradition is unmatched.

The University of Michigan football team is known as the Wolverines. Michigan has won more games (869) and holds the highest winning percentage (.745) in **National Collegiate Athletic Association (NCAA)** Division I-A history. Michigan's football program was established in 1879. It was the first school to make football popular west of the Appalachian Mountains. In 1887, Michigan players introduced football to the students at Notre Dame, who began their own football legacy and became one of Michigan's fiercest rivals. But Michigan's biggest rival is fellow Big Ten Conference member Ohio State. Since 1935, the Wolverines' season schedule has almost always concluded with a game against the Buckeyes. According to ESPN's "10 Greatest Sports Rivalries," the Michigan–Ohio State rivalry ranks number one.

Over the years, the Wolverines have established some pretty impressive records. As part of the Big Ten, Michigan has won or shared 42 league titles, more than any other football program in any other conference. Michigan is one of just three schools with 11 national championships, and the most of any school currently in Division I-A. It is the most televised school

(continues)

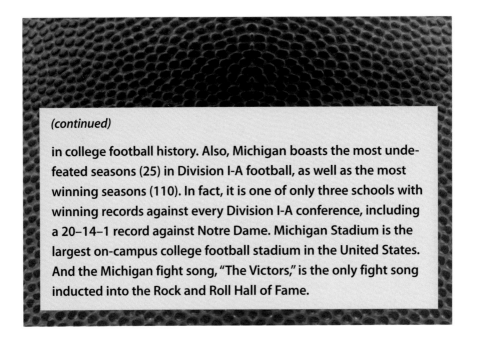

(continued)

in college football history. Also, Michigan boasts the most undefeated seasons (25) in Division I-A football, as well as the most winning seasons (110). In fact, it is one of only three schools with winning records against every Division I-A conference, including a 20–14–1 record against Notre Dame. Michigan Stadium is the largest on-campus college football stadium in the United States. And the Michigan fight song, "The Victors," is the only fight song inducted into the Rock and Roll Hall of Fame.

recruiters noticed him, and scholarship offers quickly followed. The Bradys put together a videotape of Tom's games and sent it to 55 universities. They received 52 replies. Colleges such as Southern California, UCLA, Colorado, Oregon, and Texas A&M were all in hot pursuit. The University of Michigan decided to offer a scholarship as well, perhaps sensing that a Big Ten rival might entice Tom to attend their school. Tom agreed to include a trip to Ann Arbor, Michigan, in his five allotted official visits.

At the same time, Tom was still a great catcher. He even hit a home run during a tryout with the Mariners at the Kingdome in Seattle. Ultimately, however, it was the Montreal Expos who drafted him in the eighteenth round of the 1995 Major League Baseball draft. Even though the Expos offered him a good deal of money to sign, Tom chose to stick with football because he loved the game.

Many people thought Tom would attend college on the West Coast, staying near his family and friends. His most likely choice seemed to be the University of California, Berkeley, which was just across San Francisco Bay from his hometown of San Mateo. However, his friends were not surprised when he chose Michigan. They knew he was always looking for the biggest challenge. At Michigan, Tom would compete against four or five other highly touted quarterbacks for the starting job. The school was rich in football tradition, with a 107,501-seat stadium and several national championships. Perhaps Tom's choice echoes the passage he wrote under his senior class yearbook photo: "If you want to play with the big boys, you gotta learn to play in the tall grass."

Class Act Quarterback

When Tom Brady and his parents arrived in Michigan at the beginning of his freshman year, they stopped for dinner at a restaurant near campus. The walls were decorated with pictures of Michigan football heroes. As Brady gawked at the images of these local legends, he told his mom that he would one day be as popular. As football fans now know, his prediction came true. However, his ride to fame would prove to be a bumpy one.

Trouble had already started the summer before Brady arrived in Ann Arbor. His father got a phone call from Bill Harris, the assistant coach who had recruited Brady for the Wolverines. Harris joked that he had both good news and bad news. The good news was that he could play golf with Tom that summer. The bad news was that he was no longer a coach at Michigan. As it turned out, Harris had taken over as defensive coordinator at Stanford University in nearby Palo Alto, California. The following month, Michigan head coach Gary Moeller and his wife took part in a bizarre saloon party, and Moeller was fired for his wild behavior. Just a few months after Brady had signed his letter of intent, both coaches who wanted him to attend Michigan were suddenly gone. "And he [was] screwed," Tom Sr. said in *Moving the Chains*. "But he didn't know how screwed he was."

STRUGGLING TO PROVE HIMSELF

The new head coach was Lloyd Carr, a longtime resident of Michigan, who was an all-state quarterback at Riverview Community High School. After high school, Carr left the state of Michigan to play at the University of Missouri. He stayed there just long enough to play backup quarterback on the team that won the 1966 Sugar Bowl. Carr then transferred to Northern Michigan University. After he graduated in 1968, he coached at a number of Michigan high schools and served as an assistant at both Eastern Michigan and Illinois. He joined the football staff at Michigan in 1980.

Carr got his first glimpse of Brady in a scrimmage before the 1995 season. The defense kept **blitzing** Brady, but he could throw the ball right on the money almost every time he passed. Weighing only about 185 pounds at that time, Brady took a pretty rough beating. Carr was impressed with his competitiveness and toughness.

Brady sat out his first year at Michigan as a redshirt (a college athlete who is held out of competition for one year in order to improve his skills or because of injury). The following season, he played in only two games. In those games, he completed three out of five passes for a humble total of 26 yards. His first pass as a college quarterback was intercepted and returned for a touchdown by a UCLA **linebacker**.

Lloyd Carr became head coach of the University of Michigan football team in 1995, replacing Gary Moeller. Despite Carr's overall success at Michigan, he did not appreciate Tom Brady's talent, which led to a strained relationship between player and coach. Carr is pictured here during the Wolverines' 35-29 upset loss to Illinois in Brady's senior season.

After his redshirt freshman season, Brady thought he was ready to be the Wolverines' starting quarterback in 1997. At the start of camp, Brady was third on the depth chart behind Scott Dreisbach—the starting quarterback—and the backup, Brian Griese, who would also later play in the NFL. Griese's father was Bob Griese—the star quarterback for the Miami Dolphins during the 1970s. He helped lead the Dolphins to a perfect 17–0 record in 1972, including a 14-7 win against the Washington Redskins in Super Bowl VII. (Until Brady's New England Patriots accomplished the feat in 2007, the Dolphins were the only team in NFL history to go undefeated in a season.)

The competition to become the starting quarterback at Michigan was fierce. Brady impressed the coaches with his ability to **move the chains** and the gutsy way he would hang in the pocket knowing that he was going to be hit right after he threw the ball. His willingness to risk injury to finish the play also earned him the respect of his teammates.

With his stellar performance, Brady had clearly beaten out Dreisbach. He thought he also played well enough to beat out Griese. However, at the end of camp, Griese was selected to be Michigan's **starter**. Rumors circulated that Griese's father, who was ABC's lead college football commentator, had influenced Carr's decision. Nevertheless, Brady was stunned and disappointed. Although he did see limited action in the first four games—completing 12 of 15 passes for 103 yards—his season came to an abrupt end in early October. Prior to the Wolverines' October 4 game against Northwestern, he was hospitalized with appendicitis, which sidelined him for most of the rest of the season. While he was sidelined, he lost 30 pounds. By the time he recovered, he was weak and emotionally battered. But he was determined to win the starting quarterback **position**.

With Griese as the starter, Michigan went 12–0 in 1997. The Wolverines beat Washington State, 21-16, in the Rose Bowl, winning the school's first national championship in 49 years. Fortunately for Brady, Griese would be graduating that spring. Undoubtedly, Brady would become the starting quarterback the following year. Now, however, Brady was not sure he wanted the position. He felt perhaps the Michigan coaches were holding him back. Part of Brady's problem was that he was smarter than the people who were coaching him. Coach Carr was constantly calling him to the **sidelines** to tell him things he already knew. Brady began wondering if he should transfer to a college closer to home.

There was more to consider, though, than football. Brady had been doing well in the classroom, where he was majoring in organizational studies. He also was comfortable with his social life at Michigan—he had lots of friends and enjoyed participating in extracurricular activities. So despite his difficult relationship with the coaches, he decided he still wanted to go to school there. According to *Tom Brady: MVP*, he told Carr, "Coach, I'm going to prove to you that I'm the best quarterback you have." This decision turned out to be more important than he ever could have imagined.

COMPETING WITH A LOCAL LEGEND

Brady had patiently waited behind Brian Griese to become Michigan's starting quarterback. However, the position he thought he had secured was suddenly up for grabs when a new star quarterback arrived on campus in 1998. Drew Henson was a football phenomenon from Brighton, a town not too far from Ann Arbor. *Sports Illustrated* had even printed a story on the talented signal caller. He had a number of college coaches wooing him, including those at Michigan. There was tremendous pressure on Coach Carr to promise Henson that he would be Michigan's starting quarterback.

Before the season opener at Notre Dame, Carr said in a press conference that Henson was the most talented quarterback he had ever coached. The statement was poorly timed and inappropriate. Most football coaches try to avoid quarterback controversies, because the quarterback serves as the coach on the field and the offense revolves around him. Everyone, both

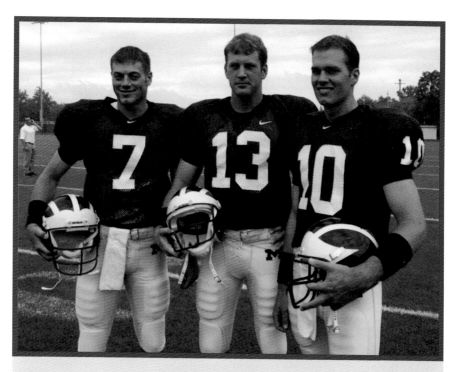

During his junior and senior seasons, Tom Brady had to share time at quarterback with Drew Henson, who was ranked as one of the top three quarterbacks in the nation coming out of Michigan's Brighton High School in 1998. Brady (right) is pictured here with Henson (left) and third-string quarterback Jason Kapsner during Michigan football media day on August 13, 1999.

coaches and teammates, invest a great deal of trust in the quarterback. Any uncertainty can throw a team off balance.

The Wolverines had a sluggish start to the 1998 season. They lost the game to Notre Dame, 36-20. Then, they followed with another loss, 38-28, to Syracuse at home. Brady threw an **interception** early in the game, and Carr immediately benched him as more than 107,000 fans cheered. Syracuse quarterback Donovan McNabb picked apart the Wolverines' defense. In the fourth quarter, Henson picked up some meaningless yardage through the air, but it was much too late to save the game. Despite the rocky start, Brady continued to start.

BRADY BREAKS INTO NOTRE DAME

In 1998, Michigan was scheduled to play its season opener at Notre Dame Stadium in South Bend, Indiana. This face-off would be no ordinary road game. A football Saturday at Notre Dame is filled with tradition, fueled by deafening cheers from crazed fans. But Tom Brady refused to get sucked into the hype and lore of such a matchup. He did, however, want to be mentally prepared for the game.

One day while driving back to Ann Arbor from Chicago, Brady stopped in South Bend to get a feel for Notre Dame Stadium. He arrived early in the evening. Much to his surprise, when he pushed on the gate to enter the stadium, it opened. Brady strolled into the deserted stadium and took a long look at the empty seats. He trudged up the stairs, row by row, probably envisioning the noisy crowd, until he reached the top. From the uppermost part of the stadium, he stared down at the field, which seemed impressive even from so far away. Then, he retraced his steps all the way back down.

He had absorbed the atmosphere and would use it in practice to help him prepare. When he got to the gate, he gave it a gentle tug. It did not budge. He tried a hard yank, but still it would not open. The gate was locked. He moved from gate to gate, but none of them would open. He wandered the stadium until dark, searching for some way out. Horrifying newspaper headlines flashed through his mind: MICHIGAN QUARTERBACK ARRESTED AT NOTRE DAME. Finally, he found a ladder, scaled the wall, and dropped safely to the ground outside. Then, he drove out of town as quickly as he could. He returned to the scene on September 5. Maybe it was punishment for his crime or just dumb luck, but the Wolverines lost, 36-20.

The Wolverines then rattled off eight straight wins, including a 27-0 drubbing of ninth-ranked Penn State. During the week before the game, Brady had been worried about moving the ball against the Nittany Lions. On the day of the game, however, he and the Michigan offense put up a season-high 360 yards in the easy win, including 224 yards through the air by Brady. This game was the first time the Nittany Lions had been shut out in 11 years. Near the end of the first half, Brady completed four passes in a row for 66 yards and a touchdown pass to wide receiver Tai Streets, who would go on to play for the San Francisco 49ers and the Detroit Lions.

Even though Michigan failed to defend its national championship, the Wolverines finished with a respectable 10–3 record and were Big Ten cochampions. Brady completed 61 percent of his passes for a total of 2,636 yards and 15 touchdowns. He also set Michigan single-game records for both attempts and completions. In a game against rival Ohio State, Brady threw the ball a record-setting 56 times. He completed 31 of the passes in the 31-16 loss to the Buckeyes.

By the end of the season, Brady felt confident that his play had silenced all the Drew Henson supporters. However, Coach Carr once again stoked the coals during preparation for the Citrus Bowl, in which Michigan faced Arkansas. The Razorbacks had a reputation for a speedy defense. This fact reignited the debate concerning who should start at quarterback for Michigan. Henson was considered more mobile than Brady. On game day, Brady drove the team into position for a field goal on Michigan's third possession. Then Carr suddenly benched Brady in favor of Henson on the next possession. Henson stayed in just long enough to make a blunder. The next possession, Brady was back in the game.

Brady played the rest of the game. Although he threw two damaging interceptions that helped Arkansas tie the game at 24-24 and then go ahead 31-24, he recovered to rally Michigan. He drove the Wolverines to two touchdowns, tying the score at 31-31 with 5:49 left in the game and then putting them up by seven a few minutes later. As it turned out, Brady's leg work made the difference on critical drives. One time, he quickly stepped out of what looked to be a sure **sack** and completed a crucial pass. Then, he ran the ball himself for a third-down conversion.

Even the Arkansas players were impressed with Brady's enthusiasm during the game. At one point in the game, Sacha Lancaster, a Razorback defensive lineman, tackled a Wolverine player. Brady held out his hand to the fallen opponent. "Good hit," he said as he pulled Lancaster to his feet. After the game, Lancaster praised Brady's sportsmanship.

The Wolverines won the game on a touchdown pass from Brady to wide receiver DiAllo Johnson with just 2:25 left in the game. Standing in the **shotgun**, Brady noticed that two opponents had lined up to cover Johnson. He figured that one of them would come after him on a blitz, leaving only one player to cover Johnson as he made his way down the sideline. His instincts were right. Brady was hit just as he threw the ball. The pass dropped into Johnson's hands, right at the **goal line** for a 21-yard touchdown. Michigan won the game, 45-31, scoring 21 points in the final six minutes.

However brief, Henson's appearance early in the game was enough to set off another quarterback controversy. The off-season was filled with stories about Henson and Brady. Henson had improved his play and was pushing for more playing time. Still, Brady's teammates seemed to stand behind him and showed it by electing him tri-captain. Even so, his teammates could do little to influence the coaching staff. Carr devised a plan for the 1999 season that would include both players. Brady would start every game, and Henson would play the second quarter. At halftime, the coaches would decide which player had earned the right to play the rest of the game.

Naturally, Brady felt hurt and betrayed. However, he could not let his confidence be shaken. For the sake of the team, he had to tell himself that when he was on the field he was the best player. Instead of letting the team become divided, Brady focused on what he needed to do to bring the players together. His attitude earned the admiration of his teammates. He approached the difficult situation with grace and class. Never once did Brady let the unfair situation affect his play or relationship with his teammates.

Brady's family, however, found it harder to restrain their emotions. By this point, Tom Sr. doubted his son would have an NFL career. He simply wanted him to have a fulfilling college career, one that he could look back on as a good experience. Much like any father, Tom was outraged at the politics taking place within the Michigan football staff. "If I'd been there . . . I would have punched Lloyd Carr in the nose," he admitted in *Moving the Chains.*

Carr's experiment lasted five weeks. Each time Henson took the field, the local fans gave him a standing ovation. With Brady taking over in the second half of most of the games, the Wolverines had a 5–0 record. They even kicked off the season with a 26-22 win over Notre Dame in Ann Arbor. In the sixth week, they played Michigan State, their in-state rival from East Lansing. For this game, Carr started Brady but turned the reins over to Henson in the second half. Henson threw an interception that led to a quick Michigan State touchdown, and the Wolverines fell behind, 27-10. In the fourth quarter, Carr put Brady back in to try to salvage what was left of the game. As usual, Brady began to move the **chains**. He nearly helped the Wolverines pull off a win, but they fell just short. He completed 30 of 41 passes for 285 yards and two touchdowns for the game, but more impressively, he connected on an amazing 18 of 20 passes for 171 yards during the Wolverines' final two scoring drives. Despite Brady's heroics, Michigan suffered its first loss of the season, 34-31.

The game against Michigan State seemed to convince all of the Michigan football players that Brady should be the starter.

No matter what kind of athletic ability Henson possessed, it was obvious that the team supported Brady. All the while, Brady kept up his positive attitude. "The way I looked at it," Brady said in *Moving the Chains*, "I was getting a chance to play, which I hadn't in my first two years. All I wanted was the opportunity, and I still had that."

Carr tested his two-quarterback system one last time. Unfortunately, it resulted in another loss for the Wolverines; this time, a 35-29 setback to Illinois at home. Although Henson had only attempted three passes in the game, Carr finally recognized that he should stick with Brady. After the game, Carr announced that Brady would be the starting quarterback for the rest of the season. The Wolverines won their last four regular-season games. The team came from behind in the last two—a tough 31-27 win at Penn State and a 24-17 victory at home over Ohio State. In the final game, Brady began running the plays he wanted to and **audibling** out of the plays he thought might not work. Although it caused some concern from the coaches, no one in the **huddle** questioned him.

THE ORANGE BOWL

For finishing 9–2 and number eight in the country, Michigan was rewarded with a berth in the Orange Bowl, where they faced fifth-ranked Alabama on New Year's Day. Most people considered the Wolverines to be the underdog. Alabama was a talented, veteran team, led by All-American running back Shaun Alexander. Michigan's best chance, according to the experts, was to hold the score down by slowing the pace of the game. At the start of the game, Alabama stacked the **line of scrimmage**, daring Brady to pass.

Brady planned to use wide receiver David Terrell as his main weapon. In the first half, he hit Terrell for 27 yards and a touchdown that cut Alabama's lead to 14-7 heading into half-time. He then hit Terrell again on a 57-yard pass play that tied the game early in the third quarter. Later, he found Terrell for a

In his senior season at Michigan, Tom Brady helped lead the Wolverines to a 10–2 record, which included a 35-34 overtime win over fifth-ranked Alabama in the Orange Bowl. In the win, Brady completed 34 of 46 passes for 369 yards and four touchdowns, three of which were to wide receiver David Terrell, who is pictured here stretching the ball over the goal line for his third touchdown of the game.

20-yard touchdown strike that pulled the Wolverines to within 28-21 after Alexander and wide receiver Freddie Millons had given the Crimson Tide a 28-14 lead. Twice, Alabama had jumped ahead by two touchdowns, and twice Brady responded. He moved the chains with short, precise passes. Alabama's defense struggled to keep up with him. For Brady, the game was so intense that he was vomiting on the sidelines between possessions.

With the game tied at 28-28, Michigan had a chance to win the game in regulation. But Alabama safety Phillip Weeks blocked Michigan kicker Hayden Epstein's 36-yard field goal attempt in the final seconds, ensuring that Michigan would play in the first overtime game in school history. In college football, games are not decided by **sudden death** like professional games. Instead, one team gets the ball on the other team's 25-yard line. Each team gets an opportunity to score. This method is repeated until one team either scores unanswered points or outscores the other team on consecutive possessions.

In this overtime contest, Michigan won the coin toss. On the very first play, Brady found **tight end** Shawn Thompson over the middle for a 25-yard touchdown. With the **extra point**, the Wolverines took a 35-28 lead. Alabama then got the ball for what could have been its only shot to win the game. On second down, Alabama quarterback Andrew Zow threw a touchdown pass to wide receiver Antonio Carter. It seemed as though the game would continue. However, Alabama kicker Ryan Pflugner pushed the extra point to the right. To the shock of many, Michigan won the Orange Bowl, 35-34.

During the game, Brady set or tied new Michigan bowl records for passing attempts, completions, yardage, and touchdowns. He threw the ball 46 times and completed 34 passes for a total of 369 yards and four touchdowns. The 2000 Orange Bowl was perhaps a turning point for Brady. He was named MVP of the game and concluded his Michigan career as one of the winningest quarterbacks in school history, going 20–5 as a starter. He also finished his career with 5,351 passing yards—at the time, he was one of only three Michigan quarterbacks to throw for more than 5,000 yards in his career. In addition, he still holds school records for most pass attempts (56, against Ohio State in 1998) and completions (34) in a game. After the game, as was the custom, the team captains led a chorus of "The Victors," the Michigan fight song. Brady's voice could clearly be heard above the rest.

The quarterback drama at Michigan would have broken the spirit of most players. But Brady was a class act. He handled the situation with determination and dignity. In the spring of 2000, the 22-year-old Brady graduated from Michigan with a business degree in organizational studies. When somebody asked about his years at the University of Michigan, Brady could have rattled off a saga of twists and turns, turmoil and heartbreak. Instead, as related in *Moving the Chains*, he thought for a moment and answered, "It was a storybook career."

Best Decision

According to *Pro Football Weekly*, Tom Brady had the negatives stacked against him as he entered the 2000 NFL draft. "Poor build. Very skinny and narrow. Ended the '99 season weighing 195 pounds and still looks like a rail at 211. Looks a little frail and lacks great physical stature and strength. Can get pushed down more easily than you'd like." The unfavorable analysis continued for several more lines. However, this review was not the first time Brady had been underestimated. He struggled in both high school and college to be noticed and appreciated. It seemed as though history was going to repeat itself once again.

SIZING UP BRADY

After his senior season, Michigan hosted NFL scouts at the college's annual Pro Day. Here, Brady caught the eye of

New Patriots head coach Bill Belichick (left) shakes hands with Owner Robert Kraft shortly before being introduced to the media at a news conference at Foxboro Stadium on January 27, 2000. Belichick and Patriots quarterbacks coach Dick Rehbein were impressed by Tom Brady's leadership skills and decided to draft the Michigan quarterback in the sixth round of the 2000 NFL draft.

Dick Rehbein, the quarterbacks coach of the New England Patriots. Rehbein and the new head coach, Bill Belichick, were looking for someone to back up Drew Bledsoe—New England's three-time Pro Bowl quarterback who led the Patriots to an appearance in Super Bowl XXXI after the 1996 season. First, Rehbein had visited Louisiana Tech University, where he checked out the rocket-armed Tim Rattay, who ultimately was drafted by the San Francisco 49ers in the seventh round of the 2000 NFL draft. Then, he traveled up to Ann Arbor.

Brady did well in the organization and leadership portions of the Wonderlic, or pro football **aptitude test**. The test asks questions such as whether or not he had ever kicked a cat and liked *Alice in Wonderland*. (The question about *Alice in Wonderland* may have been a subtle form of drug testing, because the film has some psychedelic qualities.) And, no, Brady was not a cat kicker. He was probably lucky, however, that the NFL did not ask about throwing video-game controllers. Slowly, Tom Brady's personality and football skills began to emerge. He was a polite, slender kid who threw a steady, catchable ball. He was smart, a hard worker, and other players seemed to respond to him.

Still, other teams were not convinced he had the total package, including his hometown team, the 49ers. San Francisco offensive coordinator Marty Mornhinweg pointed out that Brady had never been able to establish himself at Michigan. However, it had been impossible for Brady to do so with Coach Lloyd Carr's juggling-quarterback act. The San Diego Chargers also shied away from Brady, even though head coach Mike Riley tried to get the team to take a chance on the young quarterback.

Meanwhile, Dick Rehbein was pushing the Patriots to take the risk no one else seemed willing to take. Luckily, Bill Belichick understood there was more to a player than mere statistics. In fact, Belichick's father had been a scout and coach. He taught his son about all the intangibles that went into making a good player, beyond mere numbers. Statistics do not always measure heart or predict desire. Also, Rehbein pointed out that Michigan had gone 20–5 under Brady's leadership. Not only did Belichick listen, he was smart enough to see that Lloyd Carr's quarterback experiment actually worked in Brady's favor. During the games, Henson would go in and make mistakes. Brady would return to the game, fix the problem, and move the team into a position where it could win. Of course his attitude was commendable. But the way he took charge of the opportunities he had was what really stood out.

At the time, Belichick was not necessarily looking at Brady to be the franchise quarterback. However, Brady had worked through close games against quality competition and had managed many games well.

On April 20, 2000, the Bradys got together at their house on Portola Drive. They gathered in front of the television to watch the NFL draft on ESPN. The Brady family was optimistic and confident that Tom would get drafted, not early but certainly on the first day. The anticipation was exciting, but the process was slow. Each NFL team took its full five minutes to decide whom to pick, and the first round went on for hours. Finally, Brady decided to get out of the house and left for a San Francisco Giants baseball game. His sisters stayed home and monitored the draft on the television.

Round after round passed, but Brady's name was not called. As the draft moved on, Dick Rehbein and Bill Belichick were surprised Brady was still available. However, they also knew that most teams are not willing to draft a quarterback in the first couple of rounds, unless they know he is a can't-miss prospect. To many, Brady was not a safe draft pick. Just before the first day of the draft ended, Brady returned home from the baseball game. Obviously, he was disappointed he had not been selected during the first three rounds of the draft. However, as the picks went by on the second day of the draft, the Bradys increasingly became upset. It almost sent them over the edge when Cleveland drafted Southwest Texas State quarterback Spergon Wynn with the 183rd overall pick. In college, Wynn had completed just 47 percent of his passes compared to Brady's 62 percent. For Brady, this situation was worse than what he had experienced at Michigan. There, at least he could play his way onto the field. This time, it was not about how he played. Rather, it was about how he might play someday if he was given the chance. By the fourth round, he was getting calls from teams asking if he would like to join their team as an undrafted free agent. This offer was the kiss of death for any football player, especially a quarterback. If a player does not get drafted, he does not usually receive any kind of **signing bonus**, and thus the team does not have much of an investment in him.

The fifth round passed, and Brady fumed. He announced to his family that he was going to take a walk. On his way out, he grabbed a bat. His sisters tried to convince him that maybe it was not the best time to be carrying around a bat. But he took it anyway and pummeled anything he could find in the backyard. As the sixth round neared its conclusion, Bill Belichick leaned over and commented to his assistants that Brady should have been drafted by this point. Moments later, the telephone rang at the Brady house. Tom Sr. called his son inside to take the phone call. Finally, Brady received some good news. In the sixth round, with the 199th overall pick, he had been selected by the New England Patriots. Later that year, he agreed to a three-year contract that would pay him the league minimum of $298,000 a year plus a $38,000 signing bonus. Brady would wear number 12, and he would be penciled in as the Patriots' fourth-string quarterback, behind Bledsoe, John Friesz, and Michael Bishop.

ROOKIE SEASON

That spring, Brady reported for minicamp knowing the 2000 season would no doubt be a "redshirt" year for him. He did not expect to play much, if at all, but he was determined to look at the situation as an opportunity to prove himself yet again. One evening, he left the team's practice facility carrying a pizza. On the way out, he ran into Robert Kraft, the team's owner. Kraft is a billionaire businessman and one of the NFL's most influential owners. However, he also is a huge fan of the game. As written in *Moving the Chains*, Brady walked up to him and said, "Mr. Kraft? I'm Tom Brady. We haven't met yet, but I'm the best decision this franchise has ever made." Coming from some people, those words might have sounded arrogant. But the way Brady spoke them, they were words of confidence. Kraft was

Tom Brady warms up on the sidelines prior to the second preseason game of his career against the Detroit Lions on August 4, 2000, at the Silverdome in Pontiac, Michigan. During his rookie season, Brady did not play much, but he used the time to study the Patriots' offense and improve his physical conditioning.

not a bit offended by the comment. Before long, he would get to see Brady make good on his words.

However, Brady would first have to prove his worth to the team. His first season, Brady practiced with a group of rookie players. Almost immediately, he caught the eye of Charlie Weis, New England's offensive coordinator. Although Brady did not get many reps during practice, he did show his poise when he got the chance to run the offense. He stood out as a leader, and the players matured around him. Brady corrected the receivers when they ran the wrong route or when another player made a mistake. He understood more than just the responsibilities of his own position. He could monitor the entire offense. Throughout his rookie season, Brady was constantly watching the veteran players and taking mental notes

HOME-FIELD ADVANTAGE

What are the benefits of having a top-of-the line stadium? Quite a bit if you ask the New England Patriots. Since moving into Gillette Stadium for the 2002 season, they have experienced a good deal of success. Before 2002, Foxboro Stadium had been home to the Patriots for more than 30 years. With no premium seating and few amenities, it was one of the NFL's worst stadiums. During 1960—the Patriots' first year in the American Football League (AFL)—the team played at Nickerson Field in Boston. For the next 11 years, they played at several different stadiums in Boston, including Fenway Park, Alumni Stadium, and Harvard Stadium. Eventually, the Patriots wanted a permanent place to call home.

On September 23, 1970, construction began at a new site, 30 miles (48 kilometers) southwest of Boston—Foxborough, Massachusetts. The stadium's name was shortened to "Foxboro," and it opened just in time for the 1971 NFL season. On August 15, more than 60,000 fans filled the one tier of grandstands on both sides of the playing field and beyond each **end zone** for the Patriots' preseason opener. A single, main scoreboard hung above the seats in the south end zone. The seating was mainly composed of bleachers. However, there were some regular seating areas as well. After Robert Kraft bought the Patriots in 1993, the stadium underwent a $10 million renovation. Still, Foxboro was inadequate compared to other stadiums being of how they played. Whenever he got the chance, he made the most of his opportunity.

Daily, he strived to be the best player on the field. Weis noticed Brady's solid play and saw how he worked harder than

built at the time. When referendums for a new stadium failed to pass, Kraft decided to use his own money to begin construction on a new stadium in 2000. His vision of having a first-class stadium went a long way in helping the team. The Patriots soon emerged as Super Bowl champions, worthy of a stadium that matched their talents.

The last game played at Foxboro Stadium was during the snow-speckled night of January 19, 2002. New England defeated the Oakland Raiders, 16-13, in the divisional round of the playoffs, on their way to their first Super Bowl victory. Foxboro Stadium was demolished the following spring to make way for the new stadium. With a capacity of more than 68,000, in three decks, Gillette Stadium is a home fit for a king. The lower deck wraps around the field, while the club and upper deck levels line both sides of the gridiron—angled toward the 50-yard line for an incredible view of the action. Two massive video scoreboards hang beyond both end zones. The stadium also boasts a 120,000-square-foot clubhouse that is used year-round. The New England-like atmosphere is accented by a lighthouse design and a bridge located at the main entrance of the North Portal Plaza. After dealing with numerous issues with the grass earlier in the 2006 season, the Patriots replaced the grass with FieldTurf in time for their November 26, 2006, game with the Chicago Bears.

anyone else in the weight room. During the course of the 2000 season, he put on an additional 10 pounds of muscle. As his legs got stronger, he could take a hit better. He could stand in the pocket and complete passes even while he was being tackled. Each week, Brady prepared as if he would be the starting quarterback for the upcoming game. He wanted to be ready. For several hours each week, he routinely watched tapes of the opposition. He wanted to be familiar with their tactics, weaknesses, and strengths. On the field, a quarterback has to make split-second decisions. He wanted to be able to anticipate what a defense might do on a particular play. He tirelessly trained with Weis and Rehbein, refining the techniques that Tom Martinez had taught him years before. He studied Coach Belichick's playbook so thoroughly that he could recite many of the plays. From the sidelines, he critiqued Bledsoe's game and kept a mental log of what he did and did not do well. When Bledsoe was bothered by an injured thumb, Brady got more reps with the starters. He practiced against multiple defenses and faced an assortment of blitzes. Gradually, he became more comfortable with the other players.

Despite his dedication, Brady remained a practice player in 2000. Most weeks, he was inactive and did not even suit up. He sat out for nine games before dressing as a third-string (emergency) quarterback at Cincinnati on November 19. The rookie quarterback finally got his taste of the NFL on Thanksgiving Day, fittingly back in the state of Michigan, against the Detroit Lions. The Patriots suffered a disappointing 34-9 loss at the Silverdome. But Brady got into the game in the fourth quarter and completed one of three passes for a total of six yards. His first pass as an NFL quarterback was nearly intercepted and returned for a touchdown. The play was almost a flashback of Brady's first pass as a Wolverine, fittingly taking place in the state of Michigan. Luckily this time, the play did not result in a touchdown.

New England finished the 2000 season with a 5–11 record, good for last place in the AFC East Division. There were rumblings that Belichick's job might be on the line the following year, if he did not improve the Patriots' record. Success hung on the arm of Drew Bledsoe, who had just been given a 10-year, $103 million extension by the organization, which was then the largest contract in NFL history. The 2001 season, however, would turn out to be full of surprises.

Playing with the Big Boys

In the Patriots' locker room, it was no secret that Bill Belichick did not trust Drew Bledsoe as his starting quarterback. Both as head coach of the Cleveland Browns and as defensive coordinator with the New York Jets, Belichick had found Bledsoe to be a quarterback that opposing teams could easily scheme against. Bledsoe did not think on his toes or move quickly on them, either. Usually, he would dump the ball to the primary receiver rather than throw to his second or third reads. He took penalties and sacks at crucial moments. The Patriots' winning formula was designed on timing patterns, ball control, and defense. Drew Bledsoe did not seem to be the right fit for this football team.

During the 2001 off-season, Tom Brady dedicated himself to getting better. He even showed up for workouts he did not

Although Drew Bledsoe signed a record 10-year, $103 million contract with the Patriots after the 2000 season, Coach Bill Belichick was not entirely comfortable with him as his starting quarterback due to his inability to escape the pocket and his poor decision making. Belichick is pictured here with Bledsoe before a preseason game in 2000, the last full season Bledsoe would start for New England.

have to attend. Brady noticed that Bledsoe was not around the Patriots' facilities much; so did the coaches. For the most part, Brady stayed in Foxborough, even after the mandatory mini-camps were over. He went home to San Mateo for only a brief visit during the Fourth of July. While he was home, Brady and his father played golf as they had when Brady was growing up. At the golf club, Brady got a call from Charlie Weis on his cell phone. Weis teased Brady about slacking off and asked when he was coming back to Foxborough. Brady assured the offensive coordinator that he would be there soon. Then, as stated in *Moving the Chains*, he said, "By the way, when I come back, I'm not coming there as a backup." What Brady meant was that he was coming back to compete for the starting job.

Before the 2001 season, the Patriots signed veteran quarterback Damon Huard to serve as Bledsoe's backup after John Friesz retired. Huard's contract was worth $3 million over three years. The ousted Michael Bishop went off to NFL Europe, never to return. Much like his experience at Michigan, Brady once again had to prove himself. But he had been through this situation before. An opportunity might present itself, and then he could prove that he should be the starter.

There was one difference between New England and Michigan, however. This time, the coaches were paying attention. As Weis and Belichick watched Brady during training camp, it dawned on them that the California kid might be more than just a third-string quarterback. They thought maybe they should give Brady a chance to compete for Huard's spot.

That year's training camp turned out to be pivotal and tragic for both Brady and the Patriots. On August 6, Dick Rehbein, the only quarterbacks coach Brady had known since signing with the Patriots, died suddenly of a heart attack. Brady was devastated. Not only had he lost a friend and mentor, but Rehbein had stood firmly behind him from day one.

Nevertheless, his sorrow did not seem to affect his performance on the field. While Huard did well at camp, Brady did better. Therefore, he got more **snaps** in practice, because the coaches wanted to see him play. All players are evaluated on the same grading scale, but they are not all given the same opportunities. Some players get 50 snaps; others get 100. In the end, it was close, but Brady beat out Huard. He would be the Patriots' backup quarterback for the 2001 season. At last, Brady felt that his hard work was paying off. However, some spectators and members of the media doubted his ability. Soon, he would be put to the test; a split-second hit would spark the last great quarterback controversy of Tom Brady's career.

PROVING HIMSELF

On September 9, 2001, New England lost the first game of the season in Cincinnati to the Bengals. Two days later, al-Qaeda terrorists piloted two airplanes into the Twin Towers of the World Trade Center in New York City and one into the Pentagon, near Washington, D.C. A fourth plane, probably targeting the Capitol in Washington, D.C., spiraled into a field in Pennsylvania after passengers stormed the cockpit. The entire nation was stunned and furious at the senseless loss of life. Nearly 3,000 people lost their lives in the attacks, including the spouses of two NFL staff members.

No other entertainment enterprise in the United States was as closely tied to the country's centers of power than the NFL. Commissioner Paul Tagliabue worked in the Pentagon for three years. Even as the building still burned, he announced that the NFL would not play the following weekend. The rest of the nation's sports leagues followed the precedent set by the NFL.

The Patriots did not play again until September 23, when they lost their home opener to the New York Jets, 10-3. The game was one of the worst of Drew Bledsoe's career. On one drive, he took a delay-of-game penalty on a fourth-and-goal from the Jets' 1-yard line. Not only did the mistake cost the Patriots points, but it made Belichick and Weis look foolish for deciding not to kick an easy field goal. Then, late in the game and deep in Patriots territory, Bledsoe was chased out of the pocket and up the right sideline. New York linebacker Mo Lewis pounded Bledsoe to the ground with a vicious hit. Brady, who was standing nearby, cringed. He heard the loud smack of pads and bodies and knew it was a bad collision. Bledsoe's helmet even flew off.

Lewis's hit sheared a blood vessel in Bledsoe's chest, which filled his left chest cavity with blood. The injury must have been a frightening flashback for Bledsoe, who had nearly died as a young quarterback from a lacerated liver. He was hospitalized for almost a week. Backup quarterback Tom Brady took the field with 2:16 left in the game. He guided the Patriots down the field on an 11-play, 46-yard drive. With poise and mobility, he completed 5 of 10 passes. But the comeback fell just short after he threw three **incomplete passes** into the end zone. With the loss, New England dropped to 0–2.

Belichick was satisfied with Brady's performance, however. "All things considered, I thought in that situation he threw the ball pretty accurately and made good decisions," he said in *Greatness*. Belichick was not worried about Brady taking over as his starting quarterback. He had confidence in Brady, and the team had confidence in him, too. As for Brady, he was not a bit shaken. After all, he always prepared himself to start. He was ready for this opportunity. Those prophetic words he had penned in his high school yearbook were beginning to come to fruition—he was playing with the big boys.

A week later, Brady and the Patriots faced the Indianapolis Colts at Foxboro Stadium. In the stands, two of Brady's older sisters, Maureen and Julie, were there to cheer him on. However, the replacement quarterback did not need much encouragement during his debut as the starter. He led the Patriots to an easy 44-13 victory. He completed 13 of 23 passes for 168 yards and was sacked only once for an 11-yard loss. He lived up to the reputation he had established at Michigan: He moved the ball and did not make mistakes. Unfortunately,

Brady's step forward was erased the following week in Miami. Dolphins running back Lamar Smith nearly outgained the Patriots on his own, rushing for 144 total yards and a touchdown in Miami's 30-10 win. Meanwhile, the Miami defense limited New England to a total of 149 yards. Brady completed 12 of 24 passes for just 86 yards.

Off the field, Brady naturally settled into his leadership role. He spent hours studying film and pushed his teammates to work as hard as he did in the weight room. He spoke up in front of the team and took charge at meetings, even disagreeing with Belichick. Still, he never came across as obnoxious or cocky. He had the incredible ability to rally his team around him without giving the impression he was trying to do it.

The following week, against San Diego, Brady completed his first NFL touchdown pass, a 21-yarder to wide receiver Terry Glenn. Despite Brady's outstanding play, New England was still trailing, 26-16, with nine minutes left to play. Then, Brady began to move the chains. He led a 15-play, 69-yard drive that set up a 23-yard Adam Vinatieri field goal to cut the deficit to 26-19 with 3:31 left. Then, after the Chargers went three-and-out, Brady led an eight-play, 60-yard drive, capped by a three-yard touchdown pass to tight end Jermaine Wiggins that sent the game into overtime. All that week, Weis and Brady had practiced against one particular blitz that the San Diego defense liked to run. If Brady saw it coming, he would change the play at the line of scrimmage and throw an "out-go" ball to wide receiver David Patten. In the play, Patten would break sharply to the sideline and race straight upfield. On the first series of overtime, the Chargers failed to move the ball and were forced to **punt**. As the Patriots lined up for the first play, Brady read the blitz—the one they had spent so much time preparing for in practice. He checked off, or changed, the play. Patten adjusted his route and completely fooled Chargers **cornerback** Alex Molden, who was flagged for **pass interference** on Patten, which moved the ball to the San Diego 40-yard line.

After a few plays, the Patriots were in position for Vinatieri, who proceeded to kick the game-winning 44-yard field goal. Brady connected on 33 of 54 passes for 364 yards and two touchdowns. His performance earned him NFL Player of the Week honors. The Patriots' 29-26 overtime victory improved their record to 2–3.

New England lost only two more games the rest of the season. In game seven at Denver, Brady threw his first interception after 162 straight passes without one. He struggled in the 31-20 loss, as he was sacked two times and threw four interceptions. But Brady was resilient. He also was willing to accept responsibility for the loss. "I'm the check and balances guy out there," he explained in an interview with the *Boston Herald*, "so when there is a mix-up it's my fault."

The next loss was at home against St. Louis on November 18. The Rams' offense was led by quarterback Kurt Warner, who would win his second NFL MVP Award that season, and dual-threat running back Marshall Faulk. From 1999 to 2001, they scored more than 500 total points per season. No other team in NFL history had ever scored more than 500 points in three consecutive seasons. An offensive machine, they were known for scoring from anywhere on the field in an instant. However, the Patriots stayed close and held the Rams' potent offense to just 14 first-half points. This game carried more weight than just proving that the "Greatest Show on Turf"—the nickname given to the St. Louis offense for its record-breaking feat—was in fact beatable. It also forced Coach Belichick's hand on the most important decision of his life.

The doctors had cleared Drew Bledsoe to play prior to the game with the Rams. In the week before the game, Bledsoe and Brady shared the snaps at practice. There were benefits for using each player. Bledsoe had breathed life into a struggling franchise and had just signed a huge contract that would make it difficult to keep him on the sidelines. More important, he was the starting quarterback before his injury. There were serious

Tom Brady throws a pass during the fourth quarter of the Patriots' 29-26 overtime win against San Diego on October 14, 2001. For Brady, the game against the Chargers was a coming-out party, as he completed 33 of 54 passes for 364 yards and two touchdowns on his way to earning NFL Player of the Week honors.

rumblings within the football community about upholding the "code." According to this unwritten rule, a veteran player could not lose his job due to an injury. Bledsoe believed Belichick would honor the code and pass the reins back to him. On the other hand, Brady was winning games. He did not get sacked at inopportune times and did not throw game-killing interceptions. He helped motivate his teammates, and, during the course of the season, he had gained their trust. His confidence seemed to radiate out to every teammate.

Shortly after the St. Louis game, Belichick broke the news to Bledsoe. Brady was his starting quarterback. Suddenly, Brady was embroiled in yet another quarterback controversy. The news buzzed on the airwaves, filled the papers, and disrupted the locker room. Privately, Bledsoe was furious. But Brady focused on the job at hand, continuing to be a good teammate to everyone, including Bledsoe. St. Louis was the last game the Patriots lost. They finished the season with an impressive 11–5 record. Half of the six consecutive wins at the end of the season were tight games. Cool and poised, Brady led the Patriots right into the playoffs, which assured that Bledsoe would continue to watch from the bench. (Bledsoe was subsequently traded to the Buffalo Bills in April 2002 for a 2003 first-round draft pick.) For Brady, however, it was a time of glory. He remembered how, at Michigan, he constantly had to look over his shoulder, panning the sidelines to see if Drew Henson was slipping on his helmet. Now, he was the starter and he did not have to worry about being replaced in the middle of the game. His entire career had been building to this point; he had struggled to prove to others that he was worthy of being a starter.

More important, Brady had punched the Patriots' ticket to the playoffs. "I'm excited when we win games—individual stuff never meant much to me," Brady said as he prepared for his first NFL playoff game against the Oakland Raiders. "We're in the playoffs. It's a big step for a team. It's not about my next step; it's about our next step."

Tom Brady is hit by Raiders cornerback Charles Woodson during the fourth quarter of New England's 16-13 overtime win over Oakland in the 2001 AFC divisional playoffs. Although Brady lost the ball on the play, the officials ruled that his arm was going forward and thus it was an incomplete pass, rather than a fumble.

THE PLAYOFFS

On January 19, 2002, the Patriots met the Oakland Raiders at Foxboro Stadium in the divisional round of the playoffs. It was only Brady's fifteenth NFL game, and it turned out to be one of his most memorable. For starters, the game was played in a driving snowstorm. Brady played fairly well in the first half—he completed 6 of 13 passes for 74 yards and an interception, but the Raiders led 7-0 at halftime. In the second half, Brady led a 12-play, 62-yard drive that resulted in a 23-yard Adam Vinatieri field goal and cut the Raiders' lead to 7-3. But Oakland answered

(continues on page 61)

2001 REGULAR-SEASON RECAP

GAME 1: 9/9/01
AT CINCINNATI BENGALS
Cincinnati 23, New England 17
Record: 0–1
Quarterback: Drew Bledsoe
Bledsoe completes 22 of 38 passes for 241 yards and two touchdowns in his last full game as Patriots starting quarterback.

GAME 2: 9/23/01
AT NEW ENGLAND
New York Jets 10, New England 3
Record: 0–2
Quarterback: Drew Bledsoe/ Tom Brady
This game changes the course of the Patriots' season. With a life-threatening chest injury, veteran Drew Bledsoe leaves the game. He is replaced by backup quarterback Tom Brady, and the rest is history.

GAME 3: 9/30/01
AT NEW ENGLAND
New England 44, Indianapolis 13

Record: 1–2
Brady capably commands the Patriots to their first victory of the season, completing 13 of 23 passes for 168 yards.

GAME 4: 10/7/01
AT MIAMI DOLPHINS
Miami 30, New England 10
Record: 1–3
After taking a step forward, the Patriots take a step back, as Brady throws for just 86 yards and is sacked four times.

GAME 5: 10/14/01
AT NEW ENGLAND
New England 29, San Diego 26 (OT)
Record: 2–3
Brady guides the team to another victory in his best performance of the season. He completes 33 of 54 passes for 364 yards and two touchdowns.

GAME 6: 10/21/01
AT INDIANAPOLIS COLTS
New England 38, Indianapolis 17

Record: 3–3
Brady picks up where he left off against the Chargers, completing 16 of 20 passes for 202 yards and three touchdowns.

GAME 7: 10/28/01
AT DENVER BRONCOS
Denver 31, New England 20
Record: 3–4
New England suffers another loss after leading 20-10 in the third quarter. Up until this game, Brady had thrown an NFL record 162 straight passes without an interception. Unfortunately, he made up for it in Denver, as he threw four interceptions in the fourth quarter.

GAME 8: 11/4/01
AT ATLANTA FALCONS
New England 24, Atlanta 10
Record: 4–4
Brady rebounds from the loss to Denver by completing 21 of 31 passes for 250 yards and three touchdowns.

However, he has some help in this win; the Patriots' defense racks up nine sacks and limits the Falcons to 104 passing yards.

GAME 9: 11/11/01
AT NEW ENGLAND
New England 21, Buffalo 11
Record: 5–4
For the first time under Coach Belichick, the Patriots get above the .500 mark.

GAME 10: 11/18/01
AT NEW ENGLAND
St. Louis 24, New England 17
Record: 5–5
The "Greatest Show on Turf," led by Rams quarterback Kurt Warner, wows football fans everywhere by accumulating 401 yards through the air and three touchdowns. Although the Rams are victorious, it would be New England's last loss of the season—including their next showdown with St. Louis.

(continues)

(continued)

GAME 11: 11/25/01
AT NEW ENGLAND
New England 34, New Orleans 17
Record: 6–5
Coach Belichick announces he will be sticking with Brady, even when Bledsoe is ready to play. Brady proves it was a good decision by throwing for 258 yards and a career-high four touchdowns.

GAME 12: 12/2/01
AT NEW YORK JETS
New England 17, New York 16
Record: 7–5
Trailing 13-0, the Patriots listen carefully to Belichick's "our season is on the line" halftime speech. In the second half, the Patriots pull out all the stops, barreling past the Jets for a win.

GAME 13: 12/9/01
AT NEW ENGLAND
New England 27, Cleveland 16
Record: 8–5
The Patriots force four Browns turnovers and do not surrender an offensive touchdown in the win.

GAME 14: 12/16/01
AT BUFFALO BILLS
New England 12, Buffalo 9
Record: 9–5
Once again, the Patriots pull off an overtime win, thanks to Adam Vinatieri's 23-yard field goal.

GAME 15: 12/22/01
AT NEW ENGLAND
New England 20, Miami 13
Record: 10–5
The Patriots finish their final regular-season home game with a bang, blowing past the Dolphins in the last nonplayoff game at Foxboro Stadium.

GAME 16: 1/6/02
AT CAROLINA PANTHERS
New England 38, Carolina 6
Record: 11–5
The Patriots clinch the AFC East Division title and return two interceptions for touchdowns in the easy win.

(continued from page 57)

with two field goals of its own to increase its lead to 13-3 heading into the fourth quarter. Leading by 10 points, Oakland thought it had snuffed out New England's last flicker of hope. But Brady and the Patriots were not about to give up. Using a mostly no-huddle offense, Brady brought the Patriots back to within three points when he led a 10-play, 67-yard drive that resulted in a touchdown after he ran the ball in from six yards out.

Then the game got interesting. With just 1:50 left in the game, Brady dropped back to pass and then pulled his arm back to throw. Suddenly, Raiders cornerback Charles Woodson hit him from the blind side. The ball was knocked loose, and Oakland linebacker Greg Biekert pounced on it. However, the officials stopped the game to review the play. When referee Walt Coleman finished looking at the video replay and stepped out from under the hood, he overturned the ruling on the field. According to Coleman, Brady's arm was moving forward, and he had not tucked the ball against his body. Instead of a fumble, Brady had thrown an incomplete pass. New England kept possession, and moments later, Vinatieri nailed a 45-yard field goal to send the game into overtime.

The Patriots' good luck continued in overtime. They won the coin toss to start the extra period. Brady then drove New England 61 yards on 15 plays to put Vinatieri in position to kick a 23-yarder and win the game, 16-13. What started out as a defensive struggle had turned into a fantastic finish. Brady completed 32 of 52 passes for 312 yards in conditions more suited for the Iditarod. The second-year NFL player had the poise of a veteran. After this game, any lingering questions about a quarterback controversy were certainly squashed. Brady had proven to be The Man. And he was not done yet.

The following week, the Patriots squared off against the heavily favored Pittsburgh Steelers in the AFC Championship Game. With a little less than four minutes left in the first quarter, the Patriots were ignited by Troy Brown's 55-yard punt return for the game's first touchdown. However, after the Steelers cut the lead to 7-3, there was a moment of uncertainty for the Patriots. Late in the second quarter, Pittsburgh safety Lee Flowers rolled into Brady's left ankle, spraining it. The sprain was severe enough that Brady had to leave the game, bringing back Bledsoe for the first time since the second week of the season. Bledsoe did a good job of shaking off the rust. After taking over for Brady at the Pittsburgh 40-yard line, Bledsoe connected on three straight passes, all to David Patten, the last of which was an 11-yard touchdown. At halftime, the score stood at 14-3. Nevertheless, the story of the game was the **special teams**. During a field-goal attempt by Steelers kicker Kris Brown, Patriots **defensive end** Brandon Mitchell broke through the line and blocked the kick. Troy Brown then picked up the ball and tossed a **lateral** to safety Antwan Harris, who ran it back the last 49 yards for a touchdown. The amazing play bumped the Patriots' lead to 21-3 with just under nine minutes left in the third quarter. Despite the commanding lead, Pittsburgh quarterback Kordell Stewart led the Steelers on a pair of third-quarter touchdown drives to cut the lead to 21-17. But Vinatieri's 44-yard field goal with about 11 minutes left in the game capped the scoring, and interceptions by safeties Tebucky Jones and Lawyer Milloy sealed a 24-17 victory for the Patriots.

With a 13–5 record, the Patriots were headed to Super Bowl XXXVI. Despite Bledsoe's cameo appearance in the playoffs, Tom Brady was still the Patriots' starting quarterback. Team doctors expected his ankle to heal quickly. He would certainly be back in the starting lineup when the Patriots took on the St. Louis Rams at the Super Bowl in New Orleans the following week.

SUPER BOWL XXXVI

On February 3, 2002, the New England Patriots would again face the St. Louis Rams, this time for all the marbles. The Rams were built for speed, and the emerald turf of the Louisiana Superdome was sure to provide an advantage for the Rams' fast receivers. In addition, the Patriots would have to find a way to get to Kurt Warner, the Rams' talented quarterback. However, Brady was not worried. The 24-year-old quarterback from San Mateo, with the twinkling smile and dimpled chin, was ready to give the Rams his best shot.

As game day approached, controversy still swirled around the Patriots' camp. Aside from the Bledsoe dilemma, third-string quarterback Damon Huard, the ex-Miami Dolphin, was the only quarterback to have defeated the Kurt Warner-led Rams—twice. Still, the Patriots were confident that Brady could deliver. During the season, he had done a wonderful job of managing the team, and his charisma with the players and superb play on the field had brought tremendous success.

In 2002, the Super Bowl was delayed a week, while the NFL played out its full schedule. Back in September, the games had been postponed following the 9/11 attacks. Five months later, the nation was still on high alert. In fact, Super Bowl XXXVI was the first sporting event to be declared a "National Security Event" by President George W. Bush. Even during a typical year, security at the Super Bowl has been pretty tight.

During preparation for the Super Bowl, Belichick worked on what he perceived was a chink in the Rams' defensive armor. When the Patriots had played the Rams 11 weeks earlier, he noticed that the Rams' **defensive backs** lined up in press coverage in the red zone (the area inside the Rams' 20-yard line). If a Patriots receiver was able to get past the defensive back covering him, there would be room for Brady to complete a touchdown pass.

Finally, the big day came. Brady decided to treat this game as he would any other game. He was so relaxed before the game that he curled up in front of the lockers and took a nap while Paul McCartney sang his 9/11 tribute, "Freedom." When the two teams were about to be introduced, the public address announcer said that New England would forego individual recognition. The Patriots would be introduced "as a team." In the wake of

September 11, their decision symbolized national unity. Millions of Americans, in the crowd and watching in front of their television sets, absorbed the moment. Perhaps unintentionally, New England had made an important statement, one that described what it means to be an American—a Patriot—living in a country built on hard work and togetherness.

During the first part of the quarter, the two teams traded possessions. The Rams then opened the scoring with a little more than three minutes left in the first quarter when Warner led a 10-play, 48-yard drive that resulted in a 50-yard Jeff Wilkins field goal. The Patriots did not answer until midway through the second quarter when cornerback Ty Law intercepted a Warner pass and returned it for a 47-yard touchdown. Then the Rams self-destructed again. This time, St. Louis wide receiver Ricky Proehl fumbled the ball after he was hit by safety Antwan Harris. The ball was recovered by cornerback Terrell Buckley, who returned it 15 yards to the Rams' 40-yard line. From there, Brady drove the Patriots to the 16-yard line, with 1:12 left in the half. After throwing an incomplete pass, running back Kevin Faulk carried the ball to the 8-yard line. On the next play, Brady saw the St. Louis defensive backs do exactly what he and Belichick had predicted—line up in press coverage. Wide receiver David Patten broke to the sideline and then headed toward the end zone. Brady laid the ball up, and turning around, Patten caught it and scored a touchdown. New England ended the first half with a surprising 14-3 lead. Well, surprising to everyone except Brady.

In the second half, the Rams and Patriots traded possessions for much of the third quarter, but, once again, the Rams turned the ball over at a crucial moment. This time, cornerback Otis Smith picked off a Warner pass and set the Patriots up with good field position by returning the ball 30 yards to the Rams' 33-yard line. The Patriots could only manage a field goal, but they still bumped up their lead to 17-3, entering the fourth quarter. But the Rams showed their resilience by scoring

Tom Brady celebrates during an interview with Fox Sports commentator and NFL Hall of Famer Terry Bradshaw shortly after Brady helped lead the Patriots to a win over the St. Louis Rams in Super Bowl XXXVI. Not only was it New England's first Super Bowl victory in franchise history, but the Patriots would go on to win two more titles during the next three years.

a pair of fourth-quarter touchdowns to tie the game at 17-17. Then, with just 1:21 left on the clock, Brady and the Patriots got the ball back at their own 17-yard line. New England was out of time-outs, so Brady would be forced to go to a no-huddle offense. Throwing his trademark short-to-medium passes, Brady moved the chains. After completing three passes to running back J. R. Redmond, the Patriots had reached their own 41-yard line. Next, Brady ran a play called "64 Max All-End." The "Max" signifies that the Patriots kept both their running backs and tight ends at the line of scrimmage to protect Brady as he dropped back to pass. With just 29 seconds left, Brady decided to go downfield: He hit Troy Brown for 23 yards to set the Patriots up at the Rams' 36-yard line. Brady's pass was about neck high, but Brown—also known as Mr. Reliable—snatched the ball out of the air and ran out of bounds. The Rams' defenders read Brady's eyes and thus lost sight of Brown—but Brady did not. Brady then completed one more pass to tight end Jermaine Wiggins for six yards. He then spiked the ball with seven seconds to go. Adding a little flare, when the ball bounced back up, he caught it and balanced it on his hand for a moment before flicking it back to the ground. The game was in kicker Adam Vinatieri's hands, or rather foot, as he prepared to attempt a 48-yard field goal to win the game. He kicked the ball true and it sailed through the uprights as time expired, giving the Patriots an unlikely 20-17 victory over the St. Louis Rams. Again, Brady had saved his best for last, completing 5 of 6 passes (not including the spike) for 53 yards on the final drive. For the night, he completed 16 of 27 passes for 145 yards and a touchdown. Although his performance was not quite as impressive as Warner's 28 of 44 for 365 yards, Brady has never claimed to be a glitzy quarterback. And when he needed to step up his game, he rose to another level and made plays.

After the game, Brady stood on a podium, while sparkling confetti fell like jewels around him. Robert Kraft waved the shining Lombardi Trophy and exclaimed, "We are the Patriots, and tonight we are World Champions!" In one magical season, Brady was catapulted from rookie quarterback to national icon.

Super Bowl Superstar

From a distance, Tom Brady could sense them coming. Always alert and controlled, he seldom lowers his head or leaves himself vulnerable to blindside hits. This time, however, he was trapped. They bolted toward him with speed and force, and there was no place for him to go. No, Brady was not on the field facing an impending sack. He was just trying to eat his dinner on a Friday night.

On this particular night, Brady had made the mistake of picking a window seat. Adoring fans crowded around his booth, snapping pictures and eating fries off his plate. The restaurant manager tried to fend them off, but there were just too many of them. Outside the window, people gawked and cameras flashed. Just one year earlier, Brady had sat at the same Chili's restaurant, in the same booth, on a similar Friday night. In fact, he was a regular at that restaurant. Back then, he was just a no-name kid trying to catch a break in the NFL. Now, after an amazing storybook season, Brady was blindsided by his newfound fame. Perhaps winning the Super Bowl was the easy part.

A STAR IS BORN

Now Brady had to deal with the fame that comes with being a champion. After all, within an hour of winning the Super Bowl, Brady's picture was on the cover of a Wheaties box. His humble reaction was to comment that they should put 53 guys on the box. Likewise, when he held up the Lombardi Trophy, he said, "There's a lot of fingerprints on this."

Despite his humility, Brady was certainly going to enjoy the moment and do his fair share of celebrating. After the game, he partied with family and friends at the Fairmont Hotel in New Orleans, rubbing elbows with famous celebrities such as rap star Snoop Dogg. The next morning when he showed up for the Super Bowl MVP presentation, he wore khakis, a dark sweater, black leather jacket, and bloodshot eyes. But his sense of humor was as sharp as ever. "I didn't have a lot of sleep last night, as you can clearly see," he joked. When asked about his incredible journey that season, he said in *Greatness*, "As far as I'm concerned, it's been straight up. There hasn't been a downer yet, except this morning when the alarm went off at 6 A.M."

Still, having to get up early is a fair trade-off for the many perks that come with winning a Super Bowl. Earning the Super Bowl MVP allowed Brady to trade in his pickup for a Cadillac Escalade (a prize awarded to the MVP). It also earned him a trip to Disney World, where he filmed a commercial for the amusement park the day after winning the Super Bowl. Instead of uttering the standard line, "I'm going to Disney World," which had been stated by a number of Super Bowl MVPs, Brady said, "I'm at Disney World," in response to the question, "Where are you?"

Super Bowl XXXVI MVP Tom Brady poses with Mickey Mouse during a parade at Disney's MGM Studios on February 4, 2002. After the Patriots defeated the Rams, Brady followed tradition by heading to Disney World and filming a commercial for the amusement park.

A few weeks earlier, when he learned that he had been selected to play in the Pro Bowl, he was almost disappointed because he wanted to earn it. "It was too much too soon," Brady explained in *Greatness*. "Getting all this stuff so early . . . sometimes worries me. I've always had to work hard for everything I've ever gotten. Things don't usually come easy for me." In addition to the trips to Hawaii and Florida, there would also be countless interviews and various endorsement offers.

After returning from Disney World, Brady headed to Boston for the Patriots' victory parade. Already, fans were bedazzled with him. As his car passed by in the parade, girls threw pieces of paper with their numbers scribbled on them. Suddenly, he was playing golf in Kauai with John Elway, hanging out with Barry Bonds and Willie Mays at the San Francisco Giants' training complex in Scottsdale, Arizona, and taking mock jabs at Muhammad Ali at a charity event in Phoenix. He even accompanied Donald Trump on his private Boeing 727, where he mingled with 51 beautiful women on his way to Gary, Indiana, to judge the Miss USA 2002 pageant. However, he blew off *Vanity Fair's* exclusive Academy Awards party, because he felt he would have been out of place.

Brady realized that all the baggage that comes with being a celebrity can be distracting. Suddenly, he had to uphold his shining image—the prince of the NFL. It was a lot of pressure for a young player to handle. His biggest concern, however, was staying focused on football. Eventually, he decided to simplify his life. He turned down television appearances on *The Tonight Show with Jay Leno* and *Good Morning America*. He has politely refused most personal appearances. Also, he rejected a list of potential endorsements, including a major fast-food chain, a soft drink, grooming products, financial services companies, and car companies. Filming commercials takes time and energy. Brady wanted to save his energy for the field.

"Look, I'm a football player," Brady said in a *Sports Illustrated* interview, "and when I think back to . . . all the cool stuff I've done these last few weeks, the most fun I've had by far was winning the Super Bowl." He does not intend for any of those distractions to cause him to lose sight of what is important to him. "I *know* how I got here, and I'm going to devote myself to helping my team win it all again."

The weeks following the Super Bowl were like a whirlwind, overwhelming, yet exciting. Brady was struggling to find a balance between who he was and the celebrity he had become. He had to face the fact that he could no longer live like an average guy. People rushed him at gas stations and restaurants. He started using full service and ordering takeout. Throughout the country, young women were swooning over the football hunk. Teenage girls even showed up at his door and asked him to the prom. At the Patriots' training camp in 2001, Brady casually wheeled his suitcase up the sidewalk alone. In 2002, swarms of fans crowded around him thrusting items in front of him to autograph.

GOING FOR THE REPEAT

Brady's biggest challenge heading into the 2002 season was trying to duplicate his incredible first season. His greatest fear was becoming a "one-hit wonder." It was the same year but a new season, and the Patriots had high expectations to live up to. They lost their preseason opener to the Giants, but rebounded to win their last three practice games. The Patriots opened the season at home behind a stellar performance by Brady: He completed 29 of 43 passes for 294 yards and three touchdowns in a 30-14 win over the Pittsburgh Steelers. The following week, they easily dispatched AFC East Division foe New York, 44-7, at the Meadowlands.

The third game, against the Kansas City Chiefs, was a challenge. Still, the Patriots overcame a penalty-ridden first half to seemingly take control of the game in the fourth quarter. After New England grabbed a 38-24 lead with a little more than six minutes left, Kansas City rallied to tie the game with two touchdown runs by running back Priest Holmes, the second of which came as time expired. Any hope for a Chiefs comeback quickly faded, however. New England won the overtime coin toss, and Brady drove the Patriots' offense 53 yards on nine plays to set up a classic Vinatieri game-winning field goal.

After the win against Kansas City, the Patriots lost back-to-back games on the road to San Diego and Miami, with Brady throwing two interceptions in each game. Then, on a dreary New England Sunday, the Green Bay Packers arrived at Gillette Stadium ready for action. During the second quarter, with the Packers leading, 7-3, the New England offense became its own worst enemy. The first play of the drive, a five-yard carry by running back Antowain Smith, was brought back because of a holding penalty. The Patriots then faced first-and-20 at their own 17-yard line. After the snap, Brady tried to hit running back Kevin Faulk on a **screen pass**, but it fell incomplete. Nearly every player on both teams gave up on the play, except Packers defensive end Kabeer Gbaja-Biamila, who recovered the ball at the 8-yard line. The officials ruled that the pass was a lateral, and by rule, it was actually fumbled and a live ball. Quarterback Brett Favre then hit running back Ahman Green for a touchdown that gave the Packers a 14-3 lead heading into halftime. From that point on, the game continued to unravel for the Patriots. Green Bay's conservative passing and consistent running game resulted in a 28-10 loss for the Patriots.

The following week, the Patriots dropped their fourth straight game, falling to the Broncos, 24-16, as Brady completed only 15 of 29 passes for 130 yards. Finally, New England was able to snap the losing streak with a 38-7 victory over the Bills in their eighth game of the season. At the halfway point of the season, the defending Super Bowl champions were just 4–4. Fortunately for the Patriots, their next opponent was the 2–6 Chicago Bears. But despite Chicago's poor record, the Bears' defense kept the Patriots' offense bottled up for more than two and half quarters. But when it mattered most, Brady engineered an incredible comeback.

The Patriots trailed, 27-6, with about six minutes left in the third quarter, but then the momentum began to shift. New England's first touchdown drive of the game was an eight-play, 75-yard trip that took 3:35 off the clock. Brady was a perfect

Although the Patriots won their first three games to open the 2002 season, they lost their next four, including a 28-10 setback at home to the Green Bay Packers. In the game, Brady passed for just 183 yards, threw three interceptions, and was sacked twice. Here, Packers linebacker Na'il Diggs pressures Brady during the disappointing loss.

7 for 7 on the drive, which was capped by a 15-yard touchdown pass to running back Kevin Faulk. Then, Patriots cornerback Otis Smith intercepted a Bears pass, and the New England players began to believe they could pull out a victory. Although they had to settle for a field goal, the Patriots forced the Bears to punt on their next drive. Then, Brady led a 16-play, 54-yard scoring drive that resulted in another Vinatieri field goal.

The Patriots were still losing, 27-19, with a little more than 11 minutes left in the game. On the next Chicago possession, the Patriots again kept the Bears out of the end zone. However, they managed a 32-yard field goal, which extended their lead to 11 with about six and a half minutes left in the game. Once again, Brady responded, finding Faulk for a 36-yard touchdown. The Patriots needed only five points to tie, so they tried for the **two-point conversion**. But the attempt failed, and the Bears led, 30-25, with less than three minutes to play. Again the defense stopped the Bears, which gave the offense another chance to win.

With one time-out left and less than two minutes on the clock, Brady threw an interception to Bears defensive end Bryan Robinson. It looked as if the game was over. But Robinson had fumbled the ball and the play had to be reviewed. Luckily, the Patriots had caught a break. The officials ruled that Robinson never had possession of the ball. With just 54 seconds left, Brady got the ball back, but he faced a fourth-and-three from the Bears' 30-yard line. Brady ran for the first down and spiked the ball. After a seven-yard completion to Faulk, the Patriots called their last time-out. Then, on third-and-three with 27 seconds to go, Brady hit David Patten for a 20-yard strike just as he stepped out of the back of the end zone. Again, the play had to be reviewed to make sure he got two feet in bounds. The touchdown was good. Scoring 27 points in the second half, the Patriots pulled out a stunning 33-30 win on their last possession of the game. After the game, Brady said that he never gave up hope:

> For some reason, I just felt like we always had a shot, even though we were down 27-6. I just felt like we were still in it. [We were] just making plays there at the end . . . There's not a lot of room for error if you mess up early and you kind of put yourself behind the eight ball. But, we fought our way out of it.

The Patriots then won three of their next five games to get to 8–6 on the season. Game 15 was their last chance to secure a spot in the playoffs. But New England took a brutal 30-17 loss against the Jets. Now, the Patriots needed a little help in order to get into the playoffs. They would have to beat Miami in the final week, and the Jets would have to lose to the Packers. They came close to pulling it off.

On December 29, 2002, again against Miami, the Patriots were losing, 21-10, at halftime. After the two teams traded a couple of field goals in the second half, the score stood at 24-13, ensuring that the Patriots still needed two touchdowns to win.

TOM BRADY, THE HEARTTHROB

Millions of young women have a strong interest in Tom Brady's personal life. He has even managed to flutter the hearts of his teammates' wives. Well, here is the scoop on his romantic interests. From 2004 to 2006, Brady dated model and actress Bridget Moynahan. Moynahan starred in the ABC drama *Six Degrees* and the movie *Coyote Ugly*.

Although the relationship ended toward the end of 2006, Moynahan and Brady have a baby boy, John Edward Thomas, who was born on August 22, 2007. It was the first child for both the 36-year-old Moynahan and Brady, who flew to Los Angeles to be present for the birth of his son. Undoubtedly, with Brady's strong sense of family, he is thrilled to be a dad.

Naturally, a star quarterback will not stay single for long. Since early 2007, Brady has been dating Brazilian supermodel Gisele Bündchen, a Victoria's Secret model. She had been spotted waiting outside the Patriots' locker room at Qualcomm Stadium after New England beat San Diego, 24-21, in the divisional round of the AFC playoffs on January 14, 2007.

From 2004 to 2006, Tom Brady dated actress Bridget Moynahan. The couple is pictured here at the premier of *I Robot* in Los Angeles in July 2004.

Apparently, Brady was having some trouble with his throwing arm. Twice, he doubled over in agony after throwing a pass. Somehow, he played through the pain and led a 10-play, 68-yard touchdown drive, with a little help from a 30-yard pass interference penalty on Miami. At 24-19, the Patriots were just five points behind with 2:46 left in the game. This time, however, Brady converted the two-point conversion, throwing a three-yard touchdown pass to tight end Christian Fauria. Down by a field goal, the Patriots lined up for an **onside kick**. Instead, Vinatieri kicked the ball long, and it bounced toward the goal line. Rather than letting the ball role into the end zone, Dolphins kick returner Travis Minor picked it up but was tackled at the 4-yard line. After two incomplete passes and a seven-yard run by Dolphins quarterback Jay Fiedler, Miami was forced to punt.

Unfortunately for Miami, their punter got off a terrible kick, and the Patriots took over with 2:11 left on the clock at the Dolphins' 34-yard line. After an incomplete pass by Brady and a nine-yard run by Faulk, the Patriots faced third-and-one with two minutes left. Belichick decided to play it safe and keep the ball on the ground, but Antowain Smith was stopped for no gain. Brady then lined up as if he was going to go for it, but only to run time off the clock. Vinatieri then came on and kicked a 43-yard field goal to tie the game with 1:14 left. In overtime, New England won the toss, and Vinatieri booted the game-winning field goal to give the Patriots a 27-24 win. Sporting a 9–7 regular-season record, the Patriots' playoff hopes were briefly kept alive. But their hopes were dashed when the Jets defeated the Packers, 42-17, to clinch the playoff berth. It was a disappointing end to the 2002 season. But Brady quickly put the loss and the tough season behind him and was eager to lead the Patriots in 2003.

Recharged

Undoubtedly, the 2002 season was a letdown for Tom Brady. The 9–7 campaign ended in bitter disappointment, leaving the Patriots to regroup. Still, in some cases, Brady faired better than he did in the Patriots' Super Bowl season of 2001. He passed for more yards (3,764), more touchdowns (28), and his pass-completion percentage dipped only slightly from 63.9 to 62.1. However, sometimes more is not better—he also threw two more interceptions (14). Regardless, even though the team did not do as well, Brady actually improved.

During his first Pro Bowl trip the previous February, Brady was surrounded by some of the best players in football. He used that opportunity to record some mental notes of their specific talents. During one play of the game, Oakland Raiders quarterback Rich Gannon had receivers split out on each side of the field. He took a three-step drop and looked to throw the ball to the slant receiver. In an instant, he pumped to the right, pivoted, and then passed to his left without ever looking that way. The pass dropped into the hands of Indianapolis Colts wide receiver Marvin Harrison, who ran it 60 yards for a touchdown. When Gannon returned to the sidelines, Brady asked him how he had made that pass work. As stated in *Greatness*, Gannon answered, "Well, I've run that play a lot of times now." Gannon's answer drove home an important point for Brady. A player cannot fast-forward his career to gain experience. The experience does not come from meetings, film sessions, or practice, either. He would just have to patiently wait and learn through game situations.

Throughout 2003, Brady was growing and maturing as a quarterback. His coaches noticed a difference from year one to year three—a gradual increase in his learning curve. Many players improve dramatically in one particular area. With Brady, each aspect of his game would improve methodically. He was more comfortable in the pocket, more poised. During the Denver game in 2001—when Brady threw four interceptions—the Broncos' defense blitzed most of the game. But as he headed into his second and third seasons, he was able to make quick reads and avoid getting sacked when teams blitzed him. Even his mental skills were improving. He knew when to bring the ball down or throw it away, rather than make a critical mistake. Brady, too, was more confident in his game. "I'm not saying I'm the sage old veteran now, but I feel older," he said in *Greatness*. "You've got to grow up quickly. This job demands it."

Also, Brady had learned how to handle the demands of his celebrity status. Many players let fame ruin them, but Brady refused to become intoxicated with it. Sometimes, he would even drift back to a time before he embarked on his incredible journey. He would recall those days when he was a fourth-string quarterback from Michigan and no one noticed him. However, at times, he now felt out of touch with his family, even though he still talked to them fairly often. He used to call home every day. However, at one point, he found it difficult to squeeze in a phone call even once a week.

A RETURN TO GLORY

Entering the 2003 season, the Patriots were no longer the kings of the hill. They had tumbled down the mountain but were prepared for the grueling hike back up. The team featured some new players, including young linebacker Rosevelt Colvin, **fullback** Larry Centers, and receiver Bethel Johnson. However, the Patriots cut Lawyer Milloy, a hard-hitting safety from the University of Washington. Brady and Milloy were close friends. Shortly after his release, Milloy joined up with Drew Bledsoe and the Buffalo Bills, who would play New England in the season opener.

On September 7, Milloy, who was the last Bill to be introduced, danced across the field. His jig was a sign of things to come. The Bills rocked the Patriots, 31-0. It was the worst opening-day loss in franchise history. Brady threw four interceptions, one of which Milloy tipped to cornerback Nate Clements. At another point, Brady's old friend barreled through the line for a sack. Undoubtedly, Brady was angry and shaken, but he kept quiet. He knew that any negative talk would affect the morale of the team. After this game, Brady became painstakingly aware of just how fragile the team was, but he was determined to right the ship:

> A lot of times you have a game like this and the first thing is everyone goes in the tank. But that's not the way it's going to work because it just can't. In my career as a pro football player, two years ago we were 1–3 at the start and last year we were 3–0. It's important to win those games but it's also important that when you do lose early you have to come back. You have to realize where the problems lie and you have to correct them.

After a disappointing 9–7 season in 2002, Tom Brady hoped to get off to a fast start against the Buffalo Bills in the first week of the 2003 season. Unfortunately, Brady completed just 14 of 28 passes for 123 yards, while also throwing a season-high four interceptions in a 31-0 loss. Here, Brady, who is sitting next to fullback Fred McCrary, shows his disappointment while he checks the scoreboard in what was perhaps the worst game of his career.

Game two took place the following week at Philadelphia. The Patriots shook off any hangover from the Buffalo game and pummeled the Eagles, 31-10, forcing six **turnovers** and racking up seven sacks. During a six-minute span in the second quarter, Brady connected twice with tight end Christian Fauria for touchdowns. Later, he threw a 26-yarder to wide receiver Deion Branch for another touchdown. In all, he completed 30 of 44 passes for 255 yards and no interceptions.

The next week found the Patriots at home against their AFC East Division rival the New York Jets. It was a tough game, so physical that **defensive tackle** Ted Washington (leg), cornerback Ty Law (leg), and wide receiver David Patten (ankle) all left the field with injuries. However, New York was struggling with injuries, too, including quarterback Chad Pennington, who was recovering from a dislocated wrist. In his place, Vinny Testaverde took charge of the Jets' offense. Brady broke a 9-9 tie at the end of the third quarter with his only rushing touchdown of the season. He called his own number a yard from the end zone. In the fourth quarter, Testaverde threw a pass that was intercepted by rookie cornerback Asante Samuel, who ran it back for a 55-yard touchdown. The Patriots took a 23-16 win, despite only 181 yards passing from Brady.

At Washington for game four, the Patriots could not overcome four turnovers, including three Brady interceptions. The Redskins scored 14 points in the third quarter to take a 20-3 lead with a little more than 20 minutes left in the game. However, true to Brady style, the Patriots made an amazing comeback late in the game. Brady led a five-play, 71-yard drive, capped by a 29-yard touchdown pass to wide receiver David Givens with about two minutes left in the third quarter. Then, with 2:10 left in the game, Brady pulled the Patriots to within three points by leading a six-play, 68-yard drive that ended with a seven-yard touchdown pass to fullback Larry Centers. But the Patriots and Brady ran out of time. New England suffered a tough loss to drop to 2–2. However, it would be the last loss the Patriots would experience for an entire year.

For the Patriots, their amazing 15-game winning streak started the following week at home. The Patriots defeated the Tennessee Titans, 38-30, and then the New York Giants, 17-6. Next, they headed out on the road against AFC East Division foe Miami. Once again, the game would be a difficult affair. With two minutes left to play, the score was tied at 13-13. Olindo Mare, the league's second-most accurate kicker, lined up for a 35-yard field-goal attempt with less than two minutes left. To many, the game seemed as if it was over, but New England defensive lineman Richard Seymour had other ideas. He blocked the kick, sending the game into overtime. In overtime, Mare got a second chance to end it with another 35-yarder. This time, he pushed the kick to the right. On this day, luck seemed to be with the Patriots. After the Patriots failed to score on the ensuing drive, Miami got the ball back. But then Patriots cornerback Tyrone Poole intercepted a Jay Fiedler pass at the New England 18-yard line. In one play, Brady hit wide receiver Troy Brown on a slant. Brown sped past the Miami defense for an 82-yard touchdown—the team's longest reception of the season—and a 19-13 Patriots victory.

Game nine proved to be another action-packed road contest at Denver's Invesco Field. On the Patriots' second offensive play of the game, Brady fumbled the ball and the Broncos recovered. Four plays later, Denver was on the board with a 7-0 lead. However, Brady quickly recovered and hit Deion Branch for a 66-yard touchdown to tie the game with less than six minutes left in the first quarter. In the second quarter, Denver took the lead back with a field goal and another touchdown. The Patriots countered with two Vinatieri field goals, including one that came off a 63-yard kickoff return by Bethel Johnson. At halftime, the Patriots were down, 17-13.

In the second half, Brady played well, starting with a six-yard touchdown pass to tight end Daniel Graham, which gave New England a 20-17 lead with about nine minutes left in the third quarter. However, Denver answered with a 57-yard punt return by Deltha O'Neal to put them back on top, 24-20. Early in the fourth quarter, Vinatieri kicked a 28-yard field goal to bring the Patriots within one point. Then, with 2:49 left in the game, Coach Belichick made a risky call that proved to be brilliant. After three consecutive incompletions by Brady, the Patriots were forced to punt at their 1-yard line. Belichick believed that, if the Patriots punted, the Broncos would take over with great field position and would likely get at least a field goal. So instead of giving up three points or more, Belichick told his **center** to snap the ball over punter Ken Walter's head and out of the back of the end zone. The safety gave the Broncos two points and a 26-23 lead. The Patriots then had to kick the ball to the Broncos from their 20-yard line; Belickick was now counting on his defense to force a three-and-out by the Broncos. The free kick rolled all the way down to the Broncos' 15-yard line. Then, New England's defense forced Denver to punt after three plays, which gave the Patriots great field position at their own 42, with one time-out and a little more than two minutes to score. Six plays later, Brady completed an 18-yard touchdown pass to wide receiver David Givens with just 30 seconds left in the game. The extra point was good. Denver quarterback Danny Kanell then threw an interception that sealed the game for the Patriots.

After the thrilling win in Denver, the Patriots continued their dominance, running off seven more wins to close out the regular season. The Patriots entered their final game with a stellar 13–2 record and a chance for redemption against Bledsoe, Milloy, and the Buffalo Bills. This time, instead of throwing four interceptions, Brady fired four touchdown passes. For the third straight game, the Patriots scored on their opening drive. New England turned the tables on Buffalo with a shutout of their own, fittingly with the same 31-0 score. The Patriots finished the season with a 14–2 record, including 12 straight wins. After a disappointing second season, Brady and the Patriots seemed poised to make another run deep into the playoffs, as they did in 2001.

POSTSEASON GLORY

The divisional round of the AFC playoffs, on January 10, 2004, featured a contest between the Tennessee Titans and New England Patriots. The frigid day—4°F (-16°C), with a -10°F (-23°C) wind chill—would mark the coldest game in Patriots history. The thin-skinned Titans probably were not very comfortable in Gillette Stadium that day. Nonetheless, Brady gave them little time to think about how they felt, because he drove his team 69 yards on six plays during the Patriots' first drive. Barely four minutes into the game, Brady hit Bethel Johnson on a 41-yard scoring strike to cap the drive. However, the Titans responded with a six-play touchdown drive of their own to tie the score at 7-7. On the Patriots' next drive, Adam Vinatieri missed a 44-yard field goal. However, on the first play of the Titans' next drive, Patriots safety Rodney Harrison intercepted a Steve McNair pass and set Brady up at New England's 43-yard line. Brady calmly directed an 11-play, 57-yard drive, which ended in a one-yard touchdown run by **tailback** Antowain Smith. That would be it for the first-half scoring: Heading into halftime, the Patriots held a 14-7 lead over the Titans.

In the second half, McNair led a 70-yard drive to tie the game with a little less than 11 minutes left in the third quarter. Neither team scored for nearly the next 22 minutes, until New England took over in Tennessee territory with 6:40 left in the game. Brady led a short 13-yard drive that resulted in a 46-yard Vinatieri field goal to put the Patriots ahead, 17-14, with about four minutes left in the game. The Titans had one last chance. After driving to the Patriots' 33-yard line, though, McNair was called for intentional grounding and then an offensive lineman committed a holding penalty that essentially ended the scoring threat. Entering the playoffs, Tennessee was the only team in the league to record a quarterback sack in every regular-season game. However, they were unable to bring down Brady on this cold January day, and the Patriots won, 17-14, taking the first step on their drive toward another championship. Sitting at 15–2, the Patriots would host the Indianapolis Colts for the right to play in the Super Bowl.

The AFC Championship Game would be a matchup between two of the league's best quarterbacks: Tom Brady and Peyton Manning. Manning was known for his pinpoint precision, hitting wide receivers in stride with mesmerizing spirals. While Brady may not have been as fun to watch, he simply was a winner. However, Brady's quarterback rating was not nearly as impressive. (Manning even posted a perfect rating of 158.3 in the Colts' win against the Broncos in the wild-card round of the playoffs.) But when it came down to the wire, Brady knew how to lead his team to victory.

In fact, Brady faced many quarterbacks who had better statistics. For example, Steve McNair had a better **completion percentage** and had thrown for more yardage than Brady. Still, McNair lost. More important, Brady played better at Gillette Stadium. In nine home games during the 2003 season, he did not throw an interception. He rarely made mental errors and was adept at throwing the ball away if he was being pressured. He stayed cool under pressure and moved the chains with short, precise passes. In addition, the 26-year-old had already won a Super Bowl, so he knew what it took to win the big game.

The day of the AFC Championship, a light snow fell in Foxborough. Undaunted, Brady was ready for action. Once again, the Patriots scored on their opening drive. In 13 plays, they marched 65 yards, with Brady capping the drive on a seven-yard touchdown pass to Givens. Manning responded, bringing the Colts all the way to the New England 5-yard line. But his attempted pass to tight end Marcus Pollard was picked off in the end zone by safety Rodney Harrison. Then, early in the second quarter, Vinatieri kicked a 31-yard field goal, bumping up the score to 10-0. Another Manning interception led to a 25-yard Vinatieri field goal halfway through the quarter. Before the end of the half, the Patriots added two points on a safety when Colts punter Hunter Smith was forced to kick the ball out of the back of the end zone after the snap went over his head. The Colts entered halftime facing a 15-0 deficit.

Undaunted, the Colts finally got on the scoreboard early in the third quarter, when Manning led them on a 12-play, 52-yard touchdown drive that cut the lead to 15-7. But six

Tom Brady greets Colts quarterback Peyton Manning after New England's 24-14 win in the AFC Championship Game on January 18, 2004, at Gillette Stadium. Although Manning was co-MVP of the league that season, Brady outperformed him, completing 22 of 37 passes for 237 yards and a touchdown in the win.

plays and 48 yards later, Vinatieri responded with a 27-yard field goal. He split the uprights two more times in the second half for a total of five field goals, a playoff record. Meanwhile, Antowain Smith rushed for 100 yards on 22 carries, and Brady completed 22 of 37 passes (throwing one interception) for 237 yards and a touchdown. The Patriots intercepted Manning four times and forced five Colts turnovers. Manning, who had been named co-MVP that season (with McNair), posted a putrid **passer rating** of 35.5 in the game, the third worst of his career, and Brady and the Patriots defeated Indianapolis, 24-14. After not living up to expectations in 2002, New England had roared back to the summit and another Super Bowl.

Brady basked in the postseason glory, having helped the Patriots to an unbelievable feat of 14 straight wins. "To win 14 in a row . . . who does that?" Brady commented after the AFC Championship. He kept his feet on the ground, though, and focused on the next step. "And still the goal really hasn't been achieved," he continued, "so winning 14 in a row is great, but if there is not a 15th, then it's all for nothing."

SUPER BOWL XXXVIII

Perhaps the first trip to the Super Bowl had happened too fast. A first-year starting quarterback makes it all the way to the pinnacle of the sport, then is carried away by a whirlwind of stardom. This ride was different. Brady had a year to slow down, mature, and deal with his celebrity status. However, big accomplishments still remained, such as becoming the youngest quarterback to win *two* Super Bowls.

Much as they had done two years earlier, the Patriots headed out onto the field at Houston's Reliant Stadium as a team, led by veteran receiver Troy Brown. This time, their opponents, the Carolina Panthers, mimicked their signature move. The game started out more like a World Cup soccer match than a football game—the score was still tied at 0-0 with a little more than three minutes to play in the first half. During those final few minutes, however, both offenses came alive. Brady threw a pair of touchdown passes, and Carolina quarterback Jake Delhomme also started to move his team. The teams headed into halftime after Panthers kicker John Kasey booted a 50-yard field goal to cut the Patriots' lead to 14-10.

Although the fans in attendance and those watching on television may have been surprised by the fireworks on the field during the last few minutes of the first half, they were about to be subjected to another shocking event. During the halftime show, singer Janet Jackson's top was torn off by fellow singer Justin Timberlake, partially exposing her right breast. This incident caused quite a stir, and both Timberlake and Jackson were later asked to apologize publicly. Then, at the beginning of the second half of the game, play was briefly interrupted when a streaker lined up with the Panthers players as they prepared to kick the ball off to the Patriots. Chased by authorities, the man was eventually brought down with a little help from the shoulder of Patriots linebacker Matt Chatham. Despite all the commotion, play continued, but neither team scored during the third quarter.

Then, as the fourth quarter began, running back Antowain Smith ran for a two-yard touchdown to give the Patriots a 21-10 lead. The Panthers matched the drive with a touchdown of their own. They then attempted a two-point conversion, but it was no good. The score stood at 21-16 with about 13 minutes to go. The Patriots seemed as if they were going to take control of the game when Brady drove them all the way to the Carolina 9-yard line. But on third-and-goal, Brady attempted to hit tight end Christian Fauria in the end zone. Unfortunately for the Patriots, the pass was intercepted by Carolina cornerback Reggie Howard, who returned it to the 10-yard line. Four plays later, the Panthers took the lead on the longest play from the line of scrimmage in Super Bowl history—a Delhomme pass to wide receiver Muhsin Muhammad for an 85-yard touchdown. The Panthers took a 22-21 lead with 6:53 left in the game, after they again failed to convert a two-point conversion.

Trailing for the first time since their game with the Houston Texans on November 23, Brady went to work. He moved the Patriots 68 yards in 11 plays, and they regained the lead on a one-yard touchdown pass from Brady to linebacker Mike Vrabel. A successful two-point conversion left the Panthers behind by a touchdown, 29-22, with about three minutes to play. The lead was short-lived, however, as Delhomme connected with Ricky Proehl for a 12-yard touchdown pass that capped a seven-play, 80-yard drive that took just 1:43 off the clock.

The game was tied with a little more than a minute to play, but Brady had been in this position before. He had rallied the

Patriots during the fourth quarter when they were tied with Tennessee in the divisional round of the playoffs, and, under his command, the Patriots were 7–0 in overtime games. In

JOE MONTANA: MR. CLUTCH

Quarterback Joe Montana was selected by the San Francisco 49ers late in the third round (number 82 overall) of the 1979 NFL draft. Although he did not earn high marks at the NFL scouting combines, Montana would go on to become one of the best quarterbacks in NFL history. He became famous for his calm-under-pressure demeanor and last-minute, game-winning drives. Sound familiar? Of course it does. That is why so many people compare Tom Brady to Joe Montana. According to Brady, however, he still has a long way to go before he can be that great.

Much like Brady, Montana was highly regarded coming out of high school and also had to wait his turn to play in college. During his sophomore year at Notre Dame, Montana showed glimpses of the player he would become: He led the Fighting Irish to fourth-quarter comeback wins over North Carolina and Air Force. In the game against Air Force, he got called off the bench with 12 minutes left. He managed to bring Notre Dame back from a 20-point deficit and led them to a 31-30 win. As a junior, he again led two big comeback wins and added two more during his senior year.

Unbelievable comebacks became Montana's trademark; the most famous of these took place at the 1979 Cotton Bowl. Notre Dame squared off against the University of Houston in a New Year's Day game in which the temperature was just 20°F (-7°C). Montana had the flu and was suffering from hypothermia so disabling that the trainer spent halftime pumping him addition, he had been in a similar situation during the team's last Super Bowl appearance. New England started with the ball at its own 40-yard line. On first down, Brady fired an

full of bouillon to raise his body temperature. Heading into the fourth quarter, Notre Dame trailed 34-12. The Irish cut the lead to 34-20 after they returned a blocked punt for a touchdown. Then, with about four minutes left in the game, Montana ran for a touchdown and converted a two-point conversion to close the gap to 34-28. After Houston failed to convert a fourth-and-one from its own 29-yard line, Montana and the Irish took over with 28 seconds left in the game. On first down, Montana ran for 11 yards and then completed a 10-yard pass to get the ball down to the Cougars' 8-yard line with just six seconds left. After an incompletion, Montana threw an eight-yard touchdown pass to wide receiver Kris Haines with no time left on the clock, giving Notre Dame a 35-34 win over Houston.

Brady remembers watching Montana and the 49ers play on Sunday afternoons with his family. While he insists there can never be another Joe Montana, he does admit that as a quarterback he uses Montana as an example. "I'm working hard to try to become that," Brady said in a press conference prior to Super Bowl XXXVIII. "But it's going to have to take a lot more playoff games and a lot more Super Bowl wins to ever mention those two names [Montana and Brady] in the same sentence." During his 16-year career, Montana won four Super Bowls with the 49ers and was a three-time Super Bowl MVP. Brady, who has won three Super Bowls and two Super Bowl MVP awards, is well on his way to matching Montana's accomplishments.

incomplete pass to wide receiver Deion Branch. It would be the last of his 16 incomplete passes for the game. On second-down-and-10, he threw a 13-yard pass to Brown, followed by another for 20 more yards. However, an offensive pass interference call on Brown nullified the 20-yard gain. But Brown made up for the penalty by making a 13-yard catch on the next play. Brady then hooked up with tight end Daniel Graham for four yards and Branch for 17, bringing the ball to the Carolina 23 with just nine seconds left.

After the Patriots called time-out, Adam Vinatieri trotted onto the field to attempt the winning field goal. But Carolina then called time-out in an effort to ice the Pro Bowl kicker. Earlier in the game, Vinatieri had missed a 31-yard chip shot and had another kick blocked. But this time, he was ready. His 41-yarder was straight and true. He raised his fist into the air, because he knew right after the ball left his foot that the kick was good. Once again, the Patriots were Super Bowl champions, defeating the Panthers, 32-29. That night, Brady established a Super Bowl record—completing 32 of 48 passes for 354 yards and three touchdowns. His 32 completions were the most in Super Bowl history; a feat that had not even been accomplished by Marino, Montana, or Elway. After the game, offensive coordinator Charlie Weis asked: "Who would you rather have leading a two-minute drill?" The answer had become pretty obvious.

For the Patriots, it was Super Bowl déjà vu. Vinatieri kicked the game-winning field goal, Brady grabbed the Super Bowl MVP Award—and a Cadillac XLR—and Bill Belichick and team owner Robert Kraft hoisted the Lombardi Trophy while Patriots players hugged in the background. It was the same scene from two years earlier when Brady and his New England teammates upset the St. Louis Rams in New Orleans. Maybe the second time was not so different after all.

During the 2003 season, the Patriots featured one of the best defenses in league history. Although they had three Pro

Patriots kicker Adam Vinatieri kicks the game-winning 41-yard field goal with four seconds left in the game to give New England a 32-29 victory over the Carolina Panthers in Super Bowl XXXVIII. Vinatieri also kicked the game winner in the Patriots' victory against the St. Louis Rams in Super Bowl XXXVI.

Bowl players—linebacker Willie McGinest, defensive tackle Richard Seymour, and cornerback Ty Law—the defense had 42 different starters during the season. The players took pride in the fact that they were a cohesive unit that never played as individuals.

For Brady and his teammates, the Super Bowl win against the Panthers did not signal the end of an era, though. He recalled in *Greatness* the words of his equipment manager back at Michigan, who had worked at the university for many years and had seen many championship teams. When asked which ring was his favorite, he would answer, "The next one."

Triple Crown

Unlike his first Super Bowl win, after which he hobnobbed with Hollywood celebrities and went on private jet rides, Tom Brady celebrated his second Super Bowl victory in private. He took his girlfriend, actress Bridget Moynahan, on a three-week overseas vacation. After the first Super Bowl, he missed the annual golf trip with his dad. This year, he showed up. He even tagged along on a family vacation. In the meantime, endorsement offers and television appearance requests kept rolling in. Brady politely declined several invitations, including serving as a judge at a beauty pageant, a starring role on a television reality series, appearances on late-night television shows, as well as dozens of endorsement opportunities. After the first Super Bowl, he was a star-struck kid, wanting a taste of the Hollywood life. This time around, he was managing his life instead of letting others manage it for him.

He also underwent minor arthroscopic surgery on his shoulder. The injury had been kept secret during the 2003 season. However, at times, the injury caused Brady severe pain. Few people knew what he had to go through just to play. As soon as word leaked out, Patriots fans panicked. Anything that might affect that golden throwing arm was a big concern. By the time off-season training began, Brady was back in Foxborough, pain free and ready to go.

Returning to Foxborough was not like picking up where he left off, though. Before the Super Bowl, practices went so smoothly. His passes were crisp and sharp. Receivers were where they were supposed to be, and Brady and his team-mates were on the same wavelength. Everyone knew what to expect heading into the game. Even though players want everything to stay the same, the next season is always differ-ent. If one or two new players join the team, many adjust-ments have to be made.

A NEW BEGINNING

Unlike the 2003 season, Tom Brady wanted to get off to a fast start in 2004. Heading into the 2003 opener, he had been miffed about Lawyer Milloy's release. In 2004, he wanted to be mentally prepared for the season opener. The Patriots were matched up against the Indianapolis Colts, who boasted the same potent offense New England had faced the previous January in the AFC Championship Game. On September 9, 2004, however, the Colts were ready to exact some revenge against the Patriots. Without the chilly swirling snow, the Colts put together an outstanding offensive effort, totaling 446 yards, which on a typical week would be more than enough to get a win.

New England trailed 17-13 at halftime. It seemed as though Manning might get his revenge. But Brady was far from finished. During the third quarter, Brady threw two touchdown passes that gave the Patriots a 27-17 lead with 1:23 left in the quarter. However, Manning connected on another touchdown pass in the fourth quarter to bring the Colts within a field goal at 27-24. Despite the fact that Brady threw an interception on the next drive and then the Patriots fumbled a punt, New England was able to hold off the Colts for an important win to start off the new season. Brady racked up an impressive 335 passing yards and three touchdowns on the day. Most fans counted this game as the Patriots' sixteenth straight win, but for Brady and his teammates, they were 1–0.

The Patriots won their first six games before heading to Heinz Field in Pittsburgh to battle the Steelers. On that Halloween Sunday, New England scored early with a field goal, but the game quickly took a scary turn. Pro Bowler Ty Law was sidelined with an injured foot midway through the first quarter. On the next play, his replacement—Randall Gay—got burned on a 47-yard touchdown pass from Ben Roethlisberger to Plaxico Burress. Before the quarter ended, the Steelers scored two more touchdowns off Brady turnovers, plus a field goal. Just before halftime, Brady connected with David Givens for a 2-yard touchdown. The Patriots ended the half trailing by a painful 14 points.

Usually, Brady plays his best during the second half. But Halloween was offering him more tricks than treats. A fumble by Patriots running back Kevin Faulk resulted in another touchdown for Pittsburgh, and the Steelers' lead jumped to 31-10 less than two minutes into the second half. Later in the quarter, Brady led the Patriots on an 11-play, 59-yard drive, but they had to settle for a field goal. The Steelers then marched right back down the field to kick a field goal of their own to make it 34-13 heading into the fourth quarter. Brady delivered another touchdown pass to Givens with about six and a half minutes left in the game, but it was too little too late, as the Steelers won, 34-20. In a gruesome game, New England ran for just five yards and had possession of the ball for a measly

17:02. The Patriots' win streak was halted at 21 games (including postseason)—18 in a row for the regular season. After the game, Coach Belichick acknowledged the fact that his team had to improve if they hoped to stay on top of the AFC:

> It was pretty clear tonight that the Steelers were the better team. They out-coached us, they out-played us and they did a lot of things right. They certainly deserved to win. They won convincingly. We weren't very good in any phase of the game and didn't do much of anything right. Anytime you give up 34 points, especially on the road, it will be hard to win.

Belichick, Brady, and the rest of the Patriots learned from the loss and were quickly able to right the ship after the debacle in Pittsburgh. During the next six weeks, they rattled off six straight wins and outscored their opponents, 197–93. New England boasted a 12–1 record when the team traveled south to play the 2–11 Miami Dolphins. Running as smooth as a well-greased engine, Brady hit Kevin Faulk for a 31-yard touchdown in the opening possession. Even when Wes Welker's 71-yard punt return set up running back Sammy Morris's two-yard touchdown run to tie the score, there was no reason to fret. The chances of a monumental upset by the Dolphins were pretty remote. New England's Corey Dillon scored two times, once from the air and once on the ground. And when tight end Daniel Graham hauled in Brady's third touchdown pass to give the Patriots a 28-17 lead with about four minutes left in the game, any thoughts of a Dolphins comeback seemed unlikely. However, in just 1:52, Dolphins quarterback A. J. Feeley led Miami on a seven-play, 68-yard drive that cut the lead to 28-23 after they missed the two-point conversion. Instead of trying an onside kick, Miami opted to kick deep. Three plays later, Brady served up an interception that led to another Miami touchdown. Again missing the two-point conversion, the

Tom Brady is hit by Steelers defensive end Kimo von Oelhoffen after throwing a pass in New England's 34-20 loss to Pittsburgh on October 31, 2004. The win by the Steelers snapped the Patriots' 21-game winning streak. Fortunately for the Patriots, they came back and won six straight games and eight of their last nine to finish the regular season 14–2.

Dolphins pulled ahead by one point, 29-28. With a little more than a minute remaining, the Patriots had two time-outs to work with, and Brady needed a miracle comeback. That night, however, no miracles could be found. After he was sacked on first down, Brady threw an interception on the next play, and Feeley knelt on the ball twice to seal the 29-28 Miami win.

Miami was the last team New England would lose to that season. The Patriots easily defeated both the New York Jets and San Francisco 49ers to finish the regular season with a 14–2 record. And, once again, Brady and Manning would square off in the playoffs. This game, however, would not be as close as the game in 2004. The Patriots held Indianapolis to a field goal and Manning to 238 yards passing for an easy 20-3 win.

Paybacks can be rough, and Pittsburgh learned that lesson the hard way in the AFC Championship Game. On that dreadful Halloween, nearly three months earlier, Coach Belichick had been keeping track of his team's errors. He knew that the Patriots would be ready this time around. The once unbeatable rookie quarterback Ben Roethlisberger was intercepted on his first pass, which ultimately led to a 48-yard Adam Vinatieri field goal through a stiff wind. On the Steelers' next possession, running back Jerome Bettis fumbled and the Patriots recovered. Brady immediately capitalized, hitting Deion Branch for a 60-yard touchdown that deflated the crowd at Heinz Field. Pittsburgh managed to sneak in a field goal before the end of the first quarter, but the Patriots still led, 10-3. In the second quarter, Brady hooked up with Branch for a 45-yard pass, followed by a nine-yard scoring strike to a wide-open David Givens. Pittsburgh showed signs of life when Roethlisberger drove them 58 yards to the Patriots' 19-yard line. But on second down, Roethlisberger underthrew tight end Jerame Tuman, and the pass was intercepted by safety Rodney Harrison, who returned it 87 yards for a touchdown that gave the Patriots a 24-3 lead at halftime.

During the second half, the Steelers were able to get their offense going, but the Patriots seemed to answer almost every time. The Steelers opened the third quarter with a touchdown, but Brady came right back and led a seven-play, 69-yard touchdown drive that consumed more than seven and a half minutes. Pittsburgh fired back with another touchdown, closing the margin to 31-17 at the end of the third quarter. In the fourth quarter, Pittsburgh got as close as they would when Jeff Reed kicked a 20-yard field goal. New England then put the game away with another sustained drive, capped by a 31-yard Vinatieri field goal that made the score 34-20. As bad luck would have it, Roethlisberger threw another interception, which resulted in the Patriots' fifth touchdown of the day. With less than a minute left in the game, Pittsburgh was able to score one last touchdown, which made the score a bit more respectable at 41-27. With the win, the Patriots moved on to their third Super Bowl appearance in four seasons.

THE NEXT DYNASTY?

In Super Bowl XXXIX, the Patriots battled the Philadelphia Eagles. For the Eagles, it was the culmination of four years of frustration, because the team had lost in the **National Football Conference (NFC)** Championship Game each of the previous three seasons. For the Patriots, February 6, 2005, was a shot at the Triple Crown. The only other team to win three Super Bowls in four years was the Dallas Cowboys in 1992, 1993, and 1995. The history-making game took place on the banks of the St. Johns River, at Alltel Stadium in Jacksonville, Florida. A crowd of 78,125 was gathered there—the majority Eagles fans—while approximately 800 million worldwide watched on television.

Following the tradition started in New Orleans in 2002, the Patriots emerged from the smoke-filled tunnel as a team. The Eagles did the same, greeted with a much louder roar from the crowd. After a patriotic pregame show, featuring former presidents Bill Clinton and George H. W. Bush, the team captains gathered at midfield for the coin toss. Rodney Harrison called heads, but the coin landed tails. The Eagles chose to receive the ball.

Both teams had the ball four times in the first quarter, but neither team scored. Then, five minutes into the second quarter, the Eagles finally opened the scoring with a nine-play, 81-yard drive that culminated in a six-yard touchdown pass from Donovan McNabb to tight end L. J. Smith and a 7-0 Philadelphia lead. The big play in the drive was a 40-yard, over-the-middle pass to wide receiver Todd Pinkston, who made a

Linebacker Mike Vrabel hauls in a two-yard touchdown pass from Tom Brady that gave the Patriots a 14-7 lead over the Philadelphia Eagles in Super Bowl XXXIX on February 6, 2005. For Vrabel, it was his second touchdown reception of the season and helped New England earn its third Super Bowl victory in four seasons, as the Patriots defeated the Eagles, 24-21.

leaping grab. Next, it was Brady's turn. He drove the Patriots 37 yards on seven plays, finding David Givens in the right corner of the end zone for a four-yard touchdown pass to tie the game at 7-7 heading into halftime.

Brady took the Eagles' defense for a ride on the opening drive of the second half. He led the Patriots on a nine-play, 69-

yard drive that resulted in a two-yard touchdown toss to line-backer Mike Vrabel (again). This touchdown gave the Patriots a 14-7 lead. However, the Eagles were up to the challenge. McNabb drove the Eagles 74 yards in 10 plays. He hit running back Brian Westbrook over the middle for a 10-yard touch-down strike to tie the game with 3:35 left in the third quarter.

The score was still tied at the end of the third quarter, the first time this had happened in Super Bowl history. But on the Patriots' next drive, running backs Kevin Faulk and Corey Dillon combined for 34 yards rushing on a nine-play, 66-yard drive. Dillon then ran in from two yards out for the go-ahead touch-down that gave New England a 21-14 lead, with 13:44 left. The Patriots never trailed again. With 8:40 left in the game, Adam Vinatieri kicked a 22-yard field goal to put the Patriots up, 24-14. The Eagles would answer with a 13-play, 79-yard drive that ended in a McNabb 30-yard touchdown strike to wide receiver Greg Lewis with 1:48 to go. The Eagles got the ball one more time, but the Patriots pinned them at their own 4-yard line after an incredible punt by Josh Miller. On third-and-nine, McNabb's last-ditch effort was intercepted by Harrison with nine seconds left. The Patriots won the game, 24-21.

Undeniably, the New England Patriots became the NFL's new-est dynasty. Brady connected on 23 of 33 passes for 236 yard and two touchdowns. Deion Branch won the Super Bowl MVP Award (what would Brady do with another Cadillac anyway?) after an 11-catch, 133-yard performance. Meanwhile, Brady improved his career record to 9–0 in postseason games. Bill Belichick also over-took former Green Bay Packers coach Vince Lombardi with the tenth playoff victory of his career. And the Patriots now owned a gaudy 32–2 record since September 28, 2003. They also tied the Packers with nine consecutive playoff wins and established a new NFL record with their 21-game winning streak.

For Brady and the Patriots, they had again proved they were the best team in the NFL; for the third time in four years, the season ended with another Lombardi Trophy, a new set

of Super Bowl rings, and a ticker-tape parade. However, in
the world of football, the smiles, cheers, and pats on the back
quickly fade, as fog in the warm morning sunlight. Soon, it is

VINCE LOMBARDI AND HIS TROPHY

In 1970, the World Championship Game Trophy, which was
awarded to the winner of the first four Super Bowls, was
renamed the Lombardi Trophy in honor of one of the most
successful football coaches of all time. Vince Lombardi's
career began in the 1930s, when he played offensive guard
for Fordham University in New York City. There, he became
one of the famous members of the offensive line nicknamed
"The Seven Blocks of Granite." In 1939, he accepted a position as an assistant football coach at St. Cecelia High School
in Englewood, New Jersey. He served as the head coach there
from 1942 to 1946. Under Lombardi's leadership, the team
set an incredible record with 39 wins, 7 losses, and 5 ties, as
well as a winning streak of 25 games and another unbeaten
streak of 32.

In 1947, he returned to Fordham University as the freshman football and basketball coach. After one year, he became
an assistant on the varsity football team. However, the place
where he developed his basic coaching philosophy was at the
United States Military Academy, where he coached from 1949
to 1954. At West Point, he served as an assistant to the greatest college coach in the country at the time—Earl "Red" Blaik.
Blaik believed in keeping football simple—focusing on **blocking** and **tackling**—and achieving perfect execution through
constant repetition in practice. As an offensive line coach,
Lombardi became a workaholic, putting 16 to 17 hours a day
into his job.

time to prepare for a new season. Brady knew exactly what Coach Belichick meant when he said, "When next season starts, we'll start out at the bottom again."

Finally in 1954, Lombardi found his way to the NFL. The New York Giants hired him as an offensive coach. He worked with defensive coach Tom Landry, who later became the head coach of the Dallas Cowboys. With the Giants, Lombardi showed his coaching ability by helping to turn a losing team into a winning one. Before Lombardi joined the coaching staff, the Giants had lost nine out of 12 games and finished with the fewest points in the NFL. During his five years as assistant coach, the Giants did not have a losing season.

Other NFL teams started noticing Lombardi's talent. In 1959, he accepted an offer to become head coach of the Green Bay Packers. During his years with the Packers, Lombardi's passion for winning and violent temper quickly became his trademarks. The Packers had only won a single game in 1958. With Lombardi, they won seven games his first season, and, in the subsequent seasons under his leadership, they won six division titles, five NFL championships, and two Super Bowls (I and II). His tremendous success and ability to motivate his players made him one of the top coaches in league history.

Lombardi stepped down as head coach of the Packers in 1967 but served as general manager of the team in 1968 and coached the Washington Redskins the following year before retiring from football. During his 10-year NFL coaching career, he posted a record of 105–35–6 and never suffered a losing season. After his death in 1970, the football community honored the legendary football coach by naming the Super Bowl trophy after him.

Three-Peat?

Prior to the 2005 season, Tom Brady signed a six-year, $60 million contract with a $14.5 million signing bonus. He was one of the highest-paid players in professional sports. The benefits of a high-figured contract are obvious. The drawback is that it does not leave quite enough money to appease the other players. In the off-season, the Patriots lost some valuable players. Offensive lineman Joe Andruzzi signed with the Cleveland Browns. Talented cornerback Ty Law signed with the New York Jets, while linebacker Roman Phifer inked a deal with the New York Giants. Both defensive coordinator Romeo Crennel and offensive coordinator Charlie Weis left the Patriots to become head coach for the Cleveland Browns and the University of Notre Dame, respectively. Also, New England signed a new backup who had recently been released from the

San Diego Chargers, Doug Flutie—now 43 years old. Brady believed these changes would make 2005 the Patriots' most challenging season. His job as quarterback, he asserted, was not to make sure the team was better than it was in 2004 but make sure the Patriots were the best they could be in 2005.

Just before the season opener with Oakland on September 8, Brady appeared in *GQ* magazine. He was photographed in expensive leisure clothes, even sporting a yachting cap. During the photo shoot, which took place at a farm, someone handed him a goat. One of the photos in the magazine pictured Brady holding this baby goat. A picture with a goat was sure to get some jokes from his teammates. The day after that issue hit the newsstands, Brady practiced with the team. He looked up at the line of scrimmage only to discover that tackle Matt Light and center Dan Koppen had pinned the goat photo to the backs of their jerseys. No one laughed harder than Brady. The incident mirrored another prank Koppen had played on Brady after Brady had hosted an episode of *Saturday Night Live* on April 16, 2005. In one skit, Brady appeared in his underwear. After the show aired, Brady arrived at his locker only to find it had been decorated with jockey shorts.

UP AND DOWN

Brady's first touchdown pass of 2005 came with 2:05 left in the first quarter against Oakland. Up until that point, he had missed open receivers on three separate occasions, including one overthrow to Deion Branch. The touchdown came on third-down-and-eight from Oakland's 18-yard line. Branch made a sharp cut to the outside, and Brady hit him in the end zone to put New England up, 10-7. Oakland responded with a 73-yard pass to Randy Moss, a gifted and explosively athletic wide receiver. Covered by cornerback Tyrone Poole, Moss simply tapped the ball over Poole's head like a teenager playing keep away with a toddler. The touchdown put Oakland ahead,

14-10. Then, Brady hit wide receiver Tim Dwight on a five-yard pass, just in time to give the Patriots a 17-14 lead heading into halftime. In the second half, New England took control of the game with two touchdown runs by Corey Dillon. Oakland scored a meaningless touchdown with about three minutes left, and the Patriots would go on to win, 30-20.

What appeared to be a solid start to the season quickly turned in game two. New England lost, 27-17, to the Carolina Panthers. The Patriots' ground game was stymied by the Panthers, as New England rushed for just 39 yards. During the game, most of Brady's 44 passes came from the shotgun formation. In this type of offense, the quarterback typically throws the ball. Brady was good at reading coverages from this position and adapting to what the defense gave him. On this particular day, however, things were not falling into place. Late in the third quarter, Brady took a heavy hit from defensive end Mike Rucker, who came rushing toward Brady from the left side. He dipped his shoulder and delivered a vicious hit on Brady. The hard hit forced a fumble, which led to the Panthers' final touchdown.

The next week, New England was scheduled to play Pittsburgh, the team the Patriots had defeated the previous year in the AFC Championship Game. The more games a team wins, the more difficult that team's schedule becomes the following year. Likewise, teams that win less have an easier schedule. In 2005, five of New England's first eight games were against teams that had made the playoffs in the 2004 season. A second consecutive loss would put the Patriots in a difficult position right out of the gate, especially due to the fact that many experts considered New England's schedule the toughest for any defending Super Bowl champion in NFL history.

On September 25 against Pittsburgh, the running game again stalled. Brady had to throw 20 times in the first half. Worse, the Patriots suffered two critical injuries during the game. One of the players was safety Rodney Harrison, a brutal hitter who had been a key defensive player for the past two seasons. He blew out his left knee. Then, in the second quarter, running back Kevin Faulk caught a pass from Brady toward the left sideline and cut back up to the middle for a short gain. During the play, left tackle Matt Light, who had started 63 consecutive games since he was drafted in 2001, got tangled up with another player and ended up breaking his leg. For a right-handed quarterback like Brady, the left tackle is the most crucial player in pass protection. The left tackle protects the quarterback's blindside from the defensive ends. For the remainder of the season, Brady's left side would be trusted to two rookies who had played in only four NFL games between them. By the beginning of the fourth quarter, the Patriots trailed the Steelers, 13-10. Brady had been sacked three times. Then, he suddenly turned the tables on the Steelers.

His hot streak began with a deep out to David Givens on the left side for 14 yards. Next, he connected with Deion Branch for eight more. A 19-yard completion to Troy Brown landed the Patriots in Steelers territory at the 45-yard line. After a few more passes, Corey Dillon went over right end for a seven-yard touchdown to give New England a 17-13 lead. Brady completed five consecutive passes on the seven-play, 76-yard drive. The Pittsburgh defense grew flustered. The Patriots' momentum continued to grow when the Steelers could not move the ball. New England regained possession with 7:27 left, and Brady completed four more passes for 54 yards. The seven-play, 59-yard drive set up a 35-yard field goal for Vinatieri, and the lead increased to 20-13.

Then, second-year quarterback Ben Roethlisberger took advantage of a 44-yard kickoff return by Ricardo Colclough to jump-start the Steelers' offense. Roethlisberger marched the Steelers downfield 51 yards on nine plays to tie the game at 20-20 with 1:25 left to play. However, Brady was not done yet. Starting at the Patriots' 38-yard line, he completed three more passes, which made him a perfect 12 of 12 for the fourth quarter. He moved the chains just far enough for Vinatieri to work his magic with a game-winning 43-yard field goal. The kick was the eighteenth game-clinching field goal of his career, two of which came during the Patriots' Super Bowl wins. With the 23-20 victory, the Patriots bumped their record to 2–1.

After the win against the Steelers, the Patriots continued to be up and down. They were blown out by San Diego, losing 41-17. However, they bounced back for a 31-28 win against Atlanta, again overcoming a fourth-quarter tie to pull out an important win on the road. Once again, Vinatieri did the honors by kicking another game-winning field goal. The next week, New England dropped a game on the road, losing to Denver, 28-20. However, the Patriots came back the following week to beat AFC East Division rival Buffalo, 21-16, to improve to 4–3.

MANNING'S REVENGE

On November 7, New England squared off against the Indianapolis Colts at home on Monday Night Football. Once again, the Patriots struggled on the ground, rushing for just 34 yards. They also fell behind early, so Brady was playing on the fly, trying to lead the Patriots back through the air. To make matters worse, Brady injured his upper right leg during the game. It hurt when he pushed off and planted to throw. Somehow, Brady played through the pain, but it affected him for the rest of the season. Outside the team, few people knew about the injury; the Patriots have a policy of not revealing injuries, and players are not allowed to discuss them. Therefore, the public would not learn of Brady's sore leg. He could not use it as an excuse for the way the Patriots were playing, either, even though he would not have dreamed of doing so.

On the other side of the ball, Peyton Manning and the Colts were doing just what the Patriots had usually done to them. They were managing the clock with long, precise drives. During the Colts' second drive of the game, their offense took more than nine minutes to move 68 yards. Although this drive was by far the longest of the game, the Colts seemed to be in

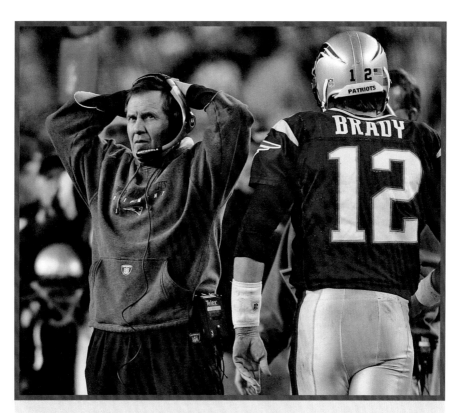

Coach Bill Belichick looks on as Tom Brady walks off the field after the Patriots fumbled the ball during the second quarter of their 40-21 loss to the Indianapolis Colts on November 7, 2005. Prior to the Colts' win, Indianapolis quarterback Peyton Manning was 0–7 in his career at New England.

control throughout. By the beginning of the third quarter, the Colts had jumped out to a 28-7 lead. However, Brady was not about to give up; he responded by guiding the Patriots on an eight-play, 73-yard drive to cut the lead in half. The Colts answered with a 35-yard field goal by Mike Vanderjagt, which made it 31-14 heading into the fourth quarter. Then another injury struck the Patriots. On fourth-and-four, Givens ran a quick slant pattern. The play was over, but Colts safety Mike Doss hit Givens late, twisting Givens's knee. Another Patriot was sidelined.

The Patriots were able to cut the lead to 34-21 in the fourth quarter, but Manning shut the door with a seven-play, 74-yard drive, capped by a 30-yard scoring strike from the Colts' quarterback to wide receiver Marvin Harrison. By the end of the game, Coach Belichick replaced Brady with Doug Flutie, and the Colts ended up taking an easy 40-21 win. And Manning, who had been 0–7 in his career at Foxborough, had gotten his revenge.

On the surface, Brady's numbers looked solid. He completed 22 of 33 passes for 265 yards and all three New England touchdowns. His quarterback rating for the game was a shining 121.4 out of a possible 158.3. Brady's statistics almost mirrored Manning's, who had completed 28 of 37 passes for 321 total yards and a rating of 117.1. Manning's quarterback rating was slightly lower due to an interception in the second quarter. However, the final score was all that mattered. The Colts rushed for 132 yards and accumulated 453 total yards to the Patriots' 288. Also, Brady noticed an attitude change on the sidelines. Everyone seemed to be using injuries as an excuse to play without passion. For the first time, his leadership skills were not working. His confidence was not carrying over to his teammates.

Toward the end of the game, Brady let his frustration get the best of him. Tight end Ben Watson dropped a pass on New England's second-to-last possession of the game. On the sidelines, Brady confronted his teammates and hurled a cup of water at the ground. Naturally, the whole outburst was caught on tape. To anyone who understood Brady's competitive nature, the incident could be dismissed. But to most football fans, rage was out of character for the calm, handsome, and controlled Tom Brady. Just the night before, Brady had appeared on *60 Minutes*, where he talked about how to stay focused in crucial moments. At the postgame press conference, Brady had little to say. "We got our butts kicked," he flatly stated. "We need to play better. We need to fight harder. . . . [The Colts] were the better team tonight."

The following Sunday, November 13, the Patriots headed south to play Miami. With the loss to Indianapolis, New England's record stood at 4–4. They really needed to win against the Dolphins. In the third quarter, with New England trailing by one, Patriots center Dan Koppen left the game with a dislocated shoulder. This injury would be another blow to the Patriots' offensive line. Brady's blindside was already being protected by two rookies. Now, veteran left **guard** Russ Hochstein would take Koppen's place. Hochstein was now playing out of position, but the Patriots had little choice.

With three minutes left to play in the game, Miami took the lead, 16-15, after Dolphins quarterback Gus Frerotte hit wide receiver Chris Chambers for a 15-yard touchdown pass. When the Patriots got the ball back, Brady came out firing. First, he completed a 59-yard pass to wide receiver Tim Dwight that got the ball down to the Dolphins' 17-yard line. Brady then prepared to go for it all, and New England drew up a play for tight end Ben Watson, who would break toward the back corner of the end zone. Brady would have to put the ball in the air long before Watson made his final move on the pattern. In this play, timing was everything. The pass was perfect. Watson made his break and plucked the ball out of the air, touching both feet down in bounds for the touchdown. New England pulled ahead, 23-16, after a two-point conversion. Even though Miami almost scored on a 70-yard drive that ended on the Patriots' 5-yard line, the New England defense stiffened and held the Dolphins out of the end zone. It was the twenty-first time in Brady's career that he quarterbacked the Patriots to a game-winning score in the fourth quarter. The following week, New England tacked on another win against New Orleans, 24-17, to boost the team's record to 6–4. A November 27 game in Kansas City brought another disappointing setback, but, as they had done throughout the season, the Patriots rebounded with a 16-3 win over the Jets on December 4.

INJURED TEAM

Around the time of the Indianapolis game, doctors diagnosed Brady with a **sports hernia**, high on his right side. The injury limited his mobility and wreaked havoc on the delicate throwing motion he had worked so hard to refine in the years since he attended Tom Martinez's camp as a youngster. Brady would need surgery, but he had to wait until the season was over. As always, the injury was kept secret from everyone outside the Patriots' locker room. Although Brady would never use it as an excuse, the hernia was the reason why his passes fluttered and sometimes ended up as interceptions.

Brady suffered another injury later in the season at Buffalo. This time, however, it occurred in plain view. Near the end of the first quarter, the Patriots took over at their own 20-yard line. Brady completed an 11-yard pass to Ben Watson for a first down. During the next eight plays, Brady connected with Watson three more times, the last pass for 14 yards to maneuver New England all the way to the Buffalo 3-yard line. On the next play, Brady called his own number, as he ran in for a 3-yard touchdown. After the snap, he took a short step back then leaped over the pile toward the end zone. As he jumped forward, a Buffalo defender slammed into his leg, cracking his left shin. He scored the touchdown but got up very slowly. Then, he limped back to the bench. The CBS cameras were glued to Brady and the Patriots' medical staff while they worked on him. After a few minutes, he stood up and took the leg for a test run. Although he was hurt, he would not miss a down. In fact, he outgained the Bills on the ground, with 17 rushing yards to their 14 yards. The Patriots picked up another win, 35-7, and were 8–5 heading into their last three games.

Throughout the season, the Patriots' locker room was like a hospital; injured players seemed to come and go. The most momentous return was in October, when linebacker Tedy Bruschi was cleared to play football again. Shortly after Super Bowl XXXIX, Bruschi collapsed from a stroke. At only 32 years old, it seemed as though his football career might be over. With his experience, though, any team would have hired him as a coach. And he already had all the money he ever needed. He came back to the game anyway. David Givens finally returned, too, against the Jets, in the Patriots' second-to-last game. Dan Koppen, still out for the season, hobbled around the locker room, while sporting a new surgical scar down the shoulder he had injured in Miami.

Of course, the injury that sparked the most discussion was the one Brady took to his left leg against Buffalo. The coaches had limited his practice time, but Brady scoffed at that precaution. Despite Brady's injury, New England played its best game of the season the following Sunday against Tampa Bay. A number of previously injured players returned for the game, and the Patriots seemed to be recovering just in time for a playoff run. They thrashed the Buccaneers, 28-0, behind 258 yards passing and three touchdowns from Brady. On a role, New England beat the Jets, but then suffered a disappointing loss against Miami, finishing the regular season with a 10–6 record. Although not as pretty as the past two seasons, it was enough to earn a **wild-card** spot in the playoffs. The two division winners in each conference with the best regular-season records get a bye in the first round of the playoffs. The other two division winners, which included the Patriots, and the two wild-card teams play in the first round of the playoffs.

STAGGERING INTO THE PLAYOFFS

The last playoff game the Patriots lost was in January 1999, when they took a beating in Jacksonville, 25-10, in the wild-card round. Three years would pass before New England would play in another playoff contest; the controversial "Tuck Rule Game" against the Oakland Raiders in the snow. Since then, they had won nine playoff games in a row with Brady as the starting quarterback. Ironically, New England would face the Jacksonville Jaguars in the wild-card round again.

The Patriots had won the AFC East Division, so they hosted the Jaguars, who had finished second to the Indianapolis Colts in the AFC South Division. Both teams got off to a slow start on a clear, cold day on the first Saturday of January. The first Patriots possession was a circus. They were penalized on the first play, and Brady's first pass of the game hit one of the referees on the head. Most of the first half was a struggle between the two defenses. Brady completed just 7 of 17 passes for 62 yards and was being pressured by the Jaguars' defensive line. Brady missed a couple of easy scoring chances, including one pass that zipped through the fingers of Deion Branch. During New England's final possession of the first quarter, Brady **scrambled** to the left on second down and gained two yards but was driven to the turf. He was then sacked on third down by linebacker Mike Peterson after the pocket collapsed. In an effort to gain some momentum, the Patriots went for it on fourth-and-10 from the Jacksonville 30. However, Brady fumbled the snap in the shotgun. He tossed the ball safely away and limped off the field.

Finally in the second quarter, the game started to turn around for the Patriots. Brady began to throw the ball better. He completed an 11-yard pass to Troy Brown for a touchdown, and the Patriots headed into halftime with a 7-3 lead. In the third quarter, Brady drove the Patriots 81 yards on 12 plays for a touchdown to Givens, bumping the lead to 14-3. On the next possession, Brady threw a 63-yard touchdown strike to Ben Watson, the longest pass play in Patriots postseason history. In the fourth quarter, cornerback Asante Samuel intercepted a Byron Leftwich pass and ran it back 73 yards for a touchdown. Samuel's pick was another one for the record books—it was the second-longest interception return in Patriots playoff history, behind the 87-yard return by Rodney Harrison in the 2004 AFC Championship Game. The game ended, 28-3, and the Patriots advanced to the divisional round of the playoffs.

The Patriots knew they would be traveling the next week, but they did not know to where. They would either play in Indianapolis, or they would play in Denver. They had lost to both teams earlier in the season. As it turned out, with Pittsburgh's win over Cincinnati, New England would play at Denver. After an uneventful first quarter, the Patriots' defense stiffened on the Broncos' initial drive of the second quarter and stopped Denver on fourth-and-one at the New England 3-yard line. Minutes later, Samuel intercepted a pass from Denver quarterback Jake Plummer, giving New England possession with a little more than six minutes left in the half. On the first play, Brady shuffled right and fired a 51-yard pass to wide receiver Andre Davis, which led to a 40-yard Vinatieri field goal.

New England's 3-0 lead would not last long, however. With two minutes remaining in the half, Kevin Faulk fumbled, and Denver recovered the ball at the New England 40-yard line. On the next play, Broncos wide receiver Ashley Lelie took off down the left sideline for a pass. Samuel ran right with him. As the pass came down, the two players got tangled and neither one was able to catch the ball. Lelie threw his arms up in frustration to draw a pass interference penalty. The questionable call gave Denver the ball at the New England 1-yard line. Plummer then handed off to running back Mike Anderson, who scored a touchdown and gave Denver a 7-3 lead. On the ensuing **kickoff**, New England kick returner Ellis Hobbs fumbled the ball at the Patriots' 39-yard line, and four plays later, Broncos kicker Jason Elam drilled a 50-yard field goal to put Denver ahead, 10-3, at halftime.

At first, the third quarter looked promising for New England. The Patriots' defense forced a three-and-out by the Broncos. Brady then drove the Patriots 58 yards in five minutes to the Denver 14-yard line. On third-and-two, he bounced an easy pass in front of Deion Branch. Instead of tying the game, New England was forced to settle for a 32-yard field goal.

Denver linebacker Al Wilson helps up Tom Brady during the Patriots' 27-13 loss to the Broncos in an AFC divisional playoff game on January 14, 2006, at Invesco Field. Not only was the loss the first for Brady in the playoffs, but it also ended the Patriots' NFL record 10-game postseason winning streak.

On the next possession, Denver failed to move the ball, and New England got another opportunity to take the lead. Brady drove the Patriots all the way to the Broncos' 10-yard line, completing passes of 33, 19, and 9 yards. Branch then caught a pass on first down, bringing the ball to the Denver 5-yard line. But on second down, David Givens dropped a Brady pass. On third down, Brady read a blitz from the Denver defense. Chased out of the pocket, he ran right. Meanwhile, Troy Brown broke out and up toward the back right corner of the end zone. Brady thought that Broncos cornerback Champ Bailey had picked up another receiver, so he passed to Brown.

Unfortunately, Bailey read the throw, intercepted the pass, and took off downfield.

On the other side of the field, tight end Ben Watson saw the interception. He set off in hot pursuit. To most, it looked as though Watson had no chance of catching Bailey. What actually occurred was an astonishing athletic feat. Watson chose the right angle and, in a high-speed sprint, he caught up to Bailey just before he reached the end zone. He hit Bailey so hard that he knocked the ball loose. Had the ball bounced out of bounds in the end zone, New England would have taken over at its own 20-yard line with a touchback. Instead, the officials ruled that the ball had gone out of bounds at the 1-yard line. Denver got a first down just shy of the Patriots' goal line. The next play resulted in a Mike Anderson touchdown, and the Broncos took a 17-6 lead. Each team would score another touchdown, but four New England turnovers led to 24 points for the Broncos. The Patriots fell, 27-13, thus ending their 2005 season and a chance to three-peat, or win their third consecutive Super Bowl. After the game, Brady was disappointed with the Patriots' effort: "When you lose, you want to go down fighting. You want to go down playing your best and we didn't do that. We made it easy for them."

Still Climbing

Tom Brady spent the 2006 off-season getting healthy. He recovered from hernia surgery, and his shin injury healed. Before the annual minicamp, he played golf with George H. W. Bush and Bill Clinton. A week later, he lost the long-driving competition at a charity golf tournament the Patriots sponsored. In reaction to his loss, Brady threw his driver into the air. Those in attendance took one look at that incident and knew Brady was ready to compete again.

Minicamp began on a June morning in Foxborough. However, some key players were missing from camp: Dan Koppen and Rodney Harrison had not fully recovered from their 2005 injuries. Deion Branch was holding out in a contract dispute. A number of familiar faces had left the team altogether. Veteran linebacker Willie McGinest was released and signed

Tom Brady tees off as former presidents George H. W. Bush (center) and Bill Clinton look on. Brady was playing with Bush and Clinton at a fund-raising event at the Cape Arundel Golf Club in Kennebunkport, Maine, on June 6, 2006.

with the Cleveland Browns. Receiver David Givens signed with the Tennessee Titans. Most surprising, however, Adam Vinatieri—the kicker who had contributed so much to the Patriots' success—signed a five-year, $12 million contract with the rival Indianapolis Colts. But Brady did not miss a beat; he worked with new receiver Reche Caldwell, who replaced Givens, and some veterans, too, such as Troy Brown and Ben Watson.

The 2006 season started off with a bang. New England only lost one of its first seven games—a 17-7 setback to the

Denver Broncos. In game eight, the Indianapolis Colts came to Gillette Stadium for the second consecutive season. The game did not start out well for New England on that Sunday in Foxborough. Brady was intercepted on the Patriots' first drive at the Indianapolis 34-yard line. Peyton Manning and the Colts capitalized on the turnover and drove 68 yards on nine plays to take a quick 7-0 lead. Early in the second quarter, Brady led the Patriots' offense on a 68-yard drive of their own, capped by a one-yard touchdown run by Corey Dillon to tie the score. The Colts, however, quickly answered with another touchdown, as rookie running back Joseph Addai scored from two yards out. Again, the Patriots answered, as Dillon scored another touchdown, this time from four yards out. Near the end of the second quarter, Adam Vinatieri, now in a Colts uniform, kicked a 23-yard field goal to give Indianapolis a 17-14 lead. With only 28 seconds remaining in the half, Brady threw his second interception of the game. Luckily, the Colts did not have enough time to score.

The second half started out in similar fashion to the first half. Dillon fumbled the ball, but this time the Colts could not take advantage of the New England turnover. However, the Colts' next drive did result in points. Manning hit Marvin Harrison on a four-yard scoring strike to give Indianapolis a 24-14 lead. On the next drive, New England's new kicker, Stephen Gostkowski, booted a 49-yard field goal to bring the Patriots within a touchdown. On the ensuing kickoff, Colts kick returner Terrence Wilkins fumbled the ball to give New England a chance to tie the game. The Patriots, though, were unable to score a touchdown, so Gostkowski came on to attempt a 36-yard field goal. With less than two minutes left in the quarter, Gostkowski's kick sailed wide right.

Both quarterbacks threw interceptions on their first possessions of the fourth quarter, first Manning, then Brady. The only difference was Indianapolis turned Brady's interception into a field goal. With a little more than 10 minutes left in the game, the Patriots trailed by 10 points, 27-17. Brady drove the Patriots' offense 43 yards to the Colts' 8-yard line, but New England would have to settle for a 26-yard field goal. After the two-minute warning, Brady threw his fourth interception, ensuring a 27-20 Patriots loss.

After dropping a 17-14 game to the New York Jets the following week, New England would go on to win six of its last seven games to close out the season. Unfortunately, the Patriots again lost to Miami, this time by the score of 21-0, as the Dolphins had beaten them in each of the last three seasons. However, with only three games left in the regular season, New England was in solid position, with a 9–4 record—much better than in 2005. On December 24, the Patriots returned to Alltel Stadium in Jacksonville for the first time since they defeated the Philadelphia Eagles in Super Bowl XXXIX. Both teams got off to a slow start, with the first quarter ending in a scoreless tie. At the start of the second quarter, New England took the lead with a 48-yard field goal. The Jaguars answered with a 74-yard touchdown run by running back Maurice Jones-Drew to pull ahead, 7-3. Then, Brady went to work. He drove the offense 82 yards on 14 plays, eating up more than seven minutes of the clock, for a touchdown that gave New England a 10-7 halftime lead.

In the second half, Brady hit tight end David Thomas for a 22-yard scoring strike and a 17-7 lead. Late in the third quarter, Jacksonville closed the gap with another Jones-Drew touchdown, making it a three-point game. Once more, the Patriots responded in the fourth quarter, as running back Laurence Maroney scored on a 27-yard touchdown run. Again, Jacksonville tightened the game with a touchdown. After the Patriots went three-and-out, Jacksonville got the ball back with less than two minutes to play and a chance to at least tie the game. But Patriots defensive lineman Jarvis Green sacked Jaguars quarterback David Garrard, forcing a fumble. The Patriots recovered the ball and celebrated a 24-21 victory.

HEADING INTO THE PLAYOFFS

The Patriots won their final game against Tennessee and finished the regular season with a 12–4 record—the same mark as Indianapolis. Baltimore and San Diego held better records, so the Patriots and Colts would both play in the wild-card round of the playoffs. New England would square off against the Jets, a team the Patriots had split their two games with during the regular season. But this time, the Patriots jumped out to an early lead and cruised to a 37-16 win.

In the divisional round, New England faced the AFC's top-seeded team, the San Diego Chargers, who had gone 14–2 in the regular season, including a perfect record at home. The Patriots were the first to score late in the first quarter with a 50-yard field goal. In the second quarter, San Diego drove 48 yards for a touchdown to take a 7-3 lead. They then scored again on a six-yard touchdown run after running back LaDainian Tomlinson caught a screen pass and ran 58 yards to set up the score. The Patriots answered with an 11-play, 72-yard scoring drive to cut the lead to 14-10 heading into halftime. After a 34-yard Gostkowski field goal cut the lead to one with a little more than two minutes left in the third quarter, Chargers quarterback Philip Rivers led his team 83 yards for a touchdown with 8:40 left in the game. The outcome looked grim for the Patriots, especially after Brady threw his third interception of the game. However, San Diego fumbled the interception and Reche Caldwell pounced on it at the San Diego 32-yard line. Five plays later, Brady hit Caldwell for a four-yard touchdown pass. A successful two-point conversion tied the game at 21. On the Patriots' next possession, Gostkowski kicked a 31-yard field goal to put the Patriots ahead, 24-21. The Chargers were able to drive into Patriots territory, but kicker Nate Kaeding missed a 54-yard field goal at the end of the game. Brady and the Patriots had advanced to another AFC Championship Game.

Tom Brady celebrates after leading the Patriots to a 24-21 win over the Chargers in an AFC divisional playoff game on January 14, 2007, at San Diego's Qualcomm Stadium. Although he threw three interceptions, Brady completed 27 of 51 passes for 280 yards and two touchdowns in the victory.

Once again, the Patriots faced their archrival—the Indianapolis Colts—but this time the game would be played at the RCA Dome in Indianapolis. New England scored first when Brady fumbled at the Indianapolis 4-yard line. Fortunately for the Patriots, the ball rolled forward and guard Logan Mankins recovered it in the end zone for a touchdown. On the next drive, ex-Patriot Adam Vinatieri kicked a 42-yard field goal. But Brady and the Patriots answered with an 11-play, 72-yard drive for a touchdown. Then, Asante Samuel intercepted a Manning pass and returned it 39 yards for a touchdown. Before halftime, Vinatieri kicked a 26-yard field goal to cut the lead to 21-6, but it must have seemed like déjà vu for the Colts.

The second half, however, was a different ball game. On their first possession, the Colts drove right down the field to cut the lead to 21-13. The Patriots then went three-and-out, and the Colts took less than three minutes to score a touchdown and pull within two points. A successful two-point conversion tied the game at 21-21. Patriots kick returner Ellis Hobbs then returned the ball all the way to the Colts' 21-yard line, and Brady quickly gave the Patriots the lead when he hit Jabar Gaffney for a six-yard touchdown pass. In the fourth quarter, the Colts fumbled at the New England 1-yard line, but center Jeff Saturday recovered the ball in the end zone for a touchdown—and another tie. Two possessions later, New England broke the tie with a 28-yard field goal. But then Adam Vinatieri answered with a field goal of his own to tie the game at 31-31. Gostkowski, however, came right back with a 43-yard field goal to put the Patriots back up, 34-31, with less than four minutes left in the game. But the Colts would finally get the best of the Patriots in the playoffs. With a little more than two minutes left, Manning led Indianapolis on a seven-play, 80-yard drive that culminated in a three-yard touchdown run by Joseph Addai. Brady's dream of another Super Bowl in 2006 was not to be. For the second straight season, the Patriots came up on the short end of the stick, losing to the Colts, 38-34.

PERFECT PATRIOTS

For the New England Patriots, the 2006 season became a distant memory when the team got off to an 8–0 start to begin the 2007 season. Heading into their Week 9 showdown with the Indianapolis Colts, the Patriots had outscored their opponents 331 to 127. In those first eight games, Tom Brady threw

30 touchdown passes, including 11 to newly acquired wide receiver Randy Moss, and was well on his way to breaking Peyton Manning's single-season touchdown record.

After the Patriots dismantled the Washington Redskins, 52-7, to improve to 8–0, Brady refused to look ahead; instead he was focused on getting better week by week: "It's been a good eight weeks . . . 8–0 is great but it really doesn't mean anything, [it] doesn't guarantee us anything. You have to keep improving through the entire season . . . I hope we perform better than we did in the first half of the season."

Brady and New England did just that: They kept their focus and not only defeated the Colts, 24-20, on November 4, but became the first NFL team since the 1972 Miami Dolphins to go undefeated during the regular season. They wrapped up their perfect season with a 38-35 win against the New York Giants on December 29. After the game, Brady credited Coach Belichick and his teammates for the Patriots' success: "Coach has kept us pretty grounded. He's not so concerned with records and stuff like that. He's most concerned with us putting our best out there each week. The veterans have responded and brought some of the younger guys along . . . It's really been a group, team-type effort."

Individually, Brady had the best season of his eight-year career. Not only did he break Manning's touchdown record with 50 touchdown passes, but he also recorded a passer rating of 117.2, which was second in NFL history to Manning's 2004 mark of 121.1. All told, Brady completed 398 of 578 passes for a Patriots record 4,806 yards (which ranks third all time in the NFL) on his way to earning his first NFL MVP Award.

From time to time, Brady has had to deal with adversity brought about by tough losses and disappointing close calls. Still, he continues climbing to new heights. As long as Brady is their quarterback, the Patriots will always be the hunted team. He accepts this challenge—not for the glory—but with the desire to be the best he can be. "What's really important to me is being a great quarterback," he said after winning his first Super Bowl. "I'm not going to let anything get in the way of that." Brady has stayed true to his word. Another Super Bowl win would put him that much closer to the ranks of Joe Montana. However, Brady is content to take it one season at a time.

TOM BRADY

Position: Quarterback

FULL NAME:
Tom Edward Brady Jr.
BORN: August 3, 1977,
San Mateo, California
HEIGHT: 6'4"

WEIGHT: 225 lbs.
COLLEGE: Michigan
TEAM:
 New England Patriots
(2000–Present)

YEAR	TEAM	G	COMP	ATT	PCT	YD	Y/A	TD	INT
2000	NE	1	1	3	33.3	6	2.0	0	0
2001	NE	15	264	413	63.9	2,843	6.9	18	12
2002	NE	16	373	601	62.1	3,764	6.3	28	14
2003	NE	16	317	527	60.2	3,620	6.9	23	12
2004	NE	16	288	474	60.8	3,692	7.8	28	14
2005	NE	16	334	530	63.0	4,110	7.8	26	14
2006	NE	16	319	516	61.8	3,529	6.8	24	12
2007	NE	16	398	578	68.9	4,806	8.3	50	8
TOTALS		112	2,294	3,642	63.0	26,370	7.2	197	86

CHRONOLOGY

1977   **August 3**   Tom Brady Jr. is born in San Mateo, California.

1993–1994   Starting quarterback at Junípero Serra High School, where he completes 219 of 441 passes (50 percent) for 3,514 yards and 33 touchdowns in two seasons.

1995   Graduates from Junípero Serra High School in spring; selected by the Montreal Expos in the eighteenth round of the Major League Baseball draft; starts freshman year at the University of Michigan in the fall and is redshirted.

1996   Plays in his first game at Michigan against UCLA.

1997   Is the Wolverines' third-string quarterback during their run to the national championship.

TIMELINE

1977
Tom Brady Jr. is born

1995
Enrolls at the University of Michigan

1999
Helps lead the Wolverines to a 10–2 record and a win in the Orange Bowl

1977   2000

1993–1994
Plays quarterback at Junípero Serra High School in San Mateo, California

1998
Helps lead Michigan to a 10–3 record, including a win in the Citrus Bowl

2000
Drafted by the New England Patriots in the sixth round (199th pick overall)

1998   Earns first start of his career in a 36-20 loss to Notre Dame on September 5; team finishes 10–3 overall (7–1 in the Big Ten) and defeats Arkansas, 45-31, in the Citrus Bowl.

1999   Helps lead Michigan to a 10–2 overall (6–2 in the Big Ten) record and a berth in the Orange Bowl.

2000   **January 1** Starting quarterback in the Orange Bowl, as Michigan battles fifth-ranked Alabama—Brady throws for 369 yards and four touchdowns to help defeat the Crimson Tide, 35-34, in overtime; finishes his career at Michigan ranked third in school history with 710 attempts and 442 completions, fourth with 5,351 yards

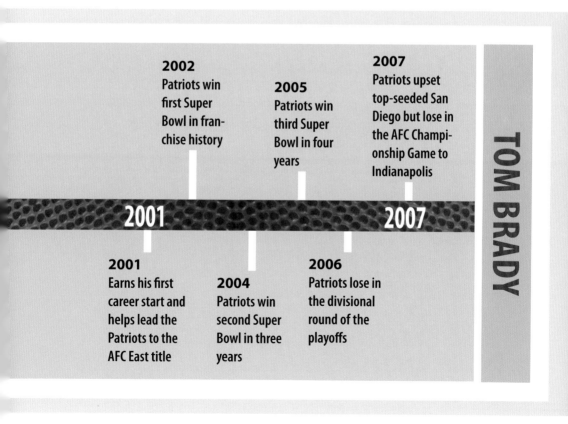

2002
Patriots win first Super Bowl in franchise history

2005
Patriots win third Super Bowl in four years

2007
Patriots upset top-seeded San Diego but lose in the AFC Championship Game to Indianapolis

2001   2007

2001
Earns his first career start and helps lead the Patriots to the AFC East title

2004
Patriots win second Super Bowl in three years

2006
Patriots lose in the divisional round of the playoffs

TOM BRADY

passing and a 62.3 completion percentage, and fifth
with 35 touchdown passes; graduates from Michigan
with a business degree in organizational studies;
drafted by the New England Patriots in the sixth
round (199th pick overall) in the NFL draft.
November 23 Plays in his first NFL game against
Detroit—completes one of three passes for six yards
in a 34-9 loss.

2001   **September 23** Starting quarterback Drew Bledsoe is
injured against the New York Jets; Brady takes over as
the Patriots' starting quarterback and completes 5 of
10 passes for 46 yards; the following week against the
Colts, he makes his first career start, completing 13 of
23 passes for 168 yards in 44-13 win; Patriots claim
sixth AFC East Division crown in franchise history.

2002   **January 19** Patriots defeat Oakland Raiders in
overtime, 16-13, in the divisional round of the AFC
playoffs, as Brady sets postseason franchise record in
attempts (52) and completions (32).
January 27 Patriots defeat Pittsburgh Steelers, 24-17,
in the AFC Championship Game, though Brady is
knocked out of the game in the second quarter.
February 3 Patriots defeat St. Louis Rams, 20–17, to
win first Super Bowl in franchise history, as Brady is
named MVP of the game.
December 29 Patriots squeeze out a 27-24 win over
Miami in an overtime thriller to finish 9–7, but
the Green Bay Packers lose to the New York Jets,
knocking the Patriots out of the playoffs.

2003   Patriots finish regular season with a 14–2 record.

2004   **January 10** Patriots beat Tennessee Titans in a close
17-14 game in the divisional round of the playoffs.
January 18 Patriots claim the AFC title, defeating the
Indianapolis Colts, 24-14.

February 1 Patriots win second Super Bowl in three years in a nail-biting 32-29 victory over the Carolina Panthers; Brady is again named Super Bowl MVP after completing 32 of 48 passes for 354 yards and three touchdowns.

For the second year in a row, the Patriots finish the regular season (2004) with a 14–2 record; Brady is named to his second Pro Bowl and records a career-high 92.6 passer rating, the second-highest mark in Patriots history.

2005   January 16 Patriots defeat the Indianapolis Colts in the divisional round of the playoffs, 20-3.

January 23 Patriots top the Pittsburgh Steelers, 41-27, securing another AFC Championship.

February 6 Patriots win their third Super Bowl in four years, defeating the Philadelphia Eagles, 24-21.

Patriots finish 2005 regular season 10–6 and win their third straight outright AFC East Division title; Brady leads the NFL with a career-high 4,110 passing yards and is named *Sports Illustrated* Sportsman of the Year.

2006   January 7 Patriots defeat the Jacksonville Jaguars, 28-3, in the wild-card round of the playoffs.

January 14 Patriots lose to Denver, 27-13, in the divisional round of the playoffs.

Patriots finish 2006 regular season 12–4 and again win the AFC East Division.

2007   January 7 Patriots defeat the New York Jets, 37-16, in the wild-card round of the playoffs.

January 14 Patriots upset the top-seeded San Diego Chargers, 24-21, in the divisional round of the playoffs, as Brady completes 27 of 51 passes for 280 yards and two touchdowns.

January 21 Patriots lose to the Indianapolis Colts, 38-34, in the AFC Championship Game.

GLOSSARY

American Football Conference (AFC)　One of the two conferences in the National Football League (NFL). The AFC was established after the NFL merged with the American Football League (AFL) in 1970.

aptitude test　A standardized test designed to predict an individual's ability to learn certain skills.

audible　A play called by the quarterback at the line of scrimmage to change the play called in the huddle.

backup　A second-string player who does not start the game, but comes in later in relief of a starter.

blitz　A defensive maneuver in which one or more linebackers or defensive backs, who normally remain behind the line of scrimmage, instead charge into the opponent's backfield.

blocking　When a player obstructs another player's path with his body. Examples: cut block, zone block, trap block, pull block, screen block, pass block, and double-team block.

bootleg　An offensive play predicated upon misdirection in which the quarterback pretends to hand the ball to another player and then carries the ball in the opposite direction of the supposed ballcarrier with the intent of either passing or running (sometimes the quarterback has the option of doing either).

center　A player position on offense. The center snaps the ball.

chain　The 10-yard-long chain that is used by the chain crew (aka, "chain gang") to measure for a new series of downs.

completion percentage　The percentage of passes thrown by a player that are completed. For example, if a running back throws one pass all season and completes it, his completion percentage would be 100 percent.

cornerback　A defensive back who lines up near the line of scrimmage across from a wide receiver. His primary job is to disrupt passing routes and to defend against short and medium passes in the passing game and to contain the rusher on running plays.

defensive back   A cornerback or safety position on the defensive team; commonly defends against wide receivers on passing plays. Generally there are four defensive backs playing at a time.

defensive end   A player position on defense who lines up on the outside of the defensive line whose principal function is to deliver pressure to the quarterback.

defensive tackle   A player position on defense on the inside of the defensive line whose principal function is to contain the run.

depth chart   A list of all the players on a team's roster, with rankings from starter to second- and third-string players; for example, Tom Brady started with the Patriots as the fourth-string quarterback but moved up to first string.

drive   A continuous set of offensive plays gaining substantial yardage and several first downs, usually leading to a scoring opportunity.

end zone   The area between the end line and the goal line, bounded by the sidelines.

extra point   A single point scored in a conversion attempt after a touchdown by place- or drop-kicking the ball through the opponent's goal.

field goal   Score of three points made by place- or drop-kicking the ball through the opponent's goal.

first down   The first of a set of four downs. Usually, a team that has a first down needs to advance the ball 10 yards to receive another first down, but penalties or field position (i.e., less than 10 yards from the opposing end zone) can affect this.

formation   An arrangement of the offensive skill players.

fourth down   The final of a set of four downs. Unless a first down is achieved or a penalty forces a replay of the down, the team will lose control of the ball after this play. If a team does not think they can get a first down, they often punt on fourth down or kick a field goal if they are close enough to do so.

fullback   A player position on offense. In modern formations, this position may be varied, and this player has more blocking responsibilities in comparison to the halfback or tailback.

fumble   A ball that a player accidentally loses possession of.

goal line   The front of the end zone.

guard   One of two player positions on offense (linemen).

handoff   A player's handing of a live ball to another player. The handoff goes either backwards or laterally, as opposed to a forward pass.

holding   There are two kinds of holding: offensive holding, illegally blocking a player from the opposing team by grabbing and holding his uniform or body; and defensive holding, called against defensive players who impede receivers who are more than five yards from the line of scrimmage, but who are not actively making an attempt to catch the ball.

huddle   An on-field gathering of members of a team in order to secretly communicate instructions for the upcoming play.

incomplete pass   A forward pass of the ball that no player legally caught.

interception   The legal catching of a forward pass thrown by an opposing player.

kickoff   A free kick that starts each half, or restarts the game following a touchdown or field goal.

lateral   A pass in football thrown parallel to the line of scrimmage or in a direction away from the opponent's goal.

line of scrimmage/scrimmage line   One of two vertical planes parallel to the goal line when the ball is to be put in play by scrimmage.

linebacker   A player position on defense. The linebackers typically play one to six yards behind the defensive linemen and are the most versatile players on the field because they can play both run and pass defense or are called to blitz.

man-to-man coverage   A defense in which all players in pass coverage, typically linebackers and defensive backs, cover a specific player.

move the chains   Using first downs to drive a team, play by play, toward their opponent's end zone.

National Collegiate Athletic Association (NCAA)   Principal governing body of college sports, including college football.

National Football Conference (NFC)   One of the two conferences in the National Football League (NFL). The NFC was established after the NFL merged with the American Football League (AFL) in 1970.

National Football League (NFL)   The largest professional American football league, with 32 teams.

offside   An infraction of the rule that requires both teams to be on their own side of their restraining line as or before the ball is put in play. Offside is typically called on the defensive team.

onside kick   A kickoff in football in which the ball travels just far enough (at least 10 yards) to be legally recovered by the kicking team.

option   A type of play in which the quarterback has the option of handing off, keeping, or laterally passing to one or more backs. Often described by a type of formation or play action, such as triple option, veer option, or counter option.

pass interference   When a player illegally hinders an eligible receiver's opportunity to catch a forward pass.

passer rating   (*also* **quarterback rating**) A numeric value used to measure the performance of quarterbacks. It was formulated in 1973 and it uses the player's completion percentage, passing yards, touchdowns, and interceptions.

play action   A tactic in which the quarterback fakes either a handoff or a throw in order to draw the defense away from the intended offensive method.

pocket   An area on the offensive side of the line of scrimmage, where the offensive linemen attempt to prevent the defensive players from reaching the quarterback during passing plays.

position   A place where a player plays relative to teammates, and/or a role filled by that player.

punt   A kick in which the ball is dropped and kicked before it reaches the ground. Used to give up the ball to the opposition after offensive downs have been used.

quarterback   An offensive player who lines up behind the center, from whom he takes the snap.

reception   When a player catches (receives) the ball.

running back   A player position on offense. Although the term usually refers to the halfback or tailback, fullbacks are also considered running backs.

sack   Tackling a ballcarrier who intends to throw a forward pass. A sack also is awarded if a player forces a fumble of the ball, or the ballcarrier to go out of bounds, behind the line of scrimmage on an apparent intended forward pass play.

safety   A player position on defense; a method of scoring (worth two points) by downing an opposing ballcarrier in his own end zone, forcing the opposing ballcarrier out of his own end zone and out of bounds, or forcing the offensive team to fumble the ball so that it exits the end zone.

salary cap   A limit on the amount any NFL team can spend on its players' salaries; the salary cap was introduced in 1994 in order to bring parity to the NFL.

scramble   On a called passing play, when the quarterback runs from the pocket in an attempt to avoid being sacked, giving the receivers more time to get open or attempting to gain positive yards by running himself.

screen pass   A forward pass in football to a receiver at or behind the line of scrimmage who is protected by a screen of blockers.

secondary   Refers to the defensive "backfield," specifically the safeties and cornerbacks.

shotgun formation   Formation in which offensive team may line up at the start of a play. In this formation, the quarterback receives the snap five to eight yards behind the center.

sideline   One of the lines marking each side of the field.

signing bonus   A onetime up-front payment for signing with a team.

snap   The handoff or pass from the center that begins a play from scrimmage.

special teams   The units that handle kickoffs, punts, free kicks, and field-goal attempts.

sports hernia   A tear in the muscles of the lower abdomen; the tear can lead to the muscle pulling away from the bones.

starter   A player who is the first to play his position within a given game or season. Depending on the position and the game situation, this player may be replaced or share time with one or more players later in the game. For example, a quarterback may start the game but be replaced by a backup quarterback if the game becomes one-sided.

sudden death   In overtime, when a team scores any points, the game ends; in sudden death, the other team does not have a chance to answer the points.

tackle   The act of forcing a ballcarrier to the ground. Also, a position on the offensive and defensive line.

tailback   Player position on offense farthest ("deepest") back, except in kicking formations.

tight end   A player position on offense, often known as a Y receiver when he lines up on the line of scrimmage, next to the offensive tackle. Tight ends are used as blockers during running plays and either run a route or stay in to block during passing plays.

time of possession   The amount of time one team has the ball in its possession relative to the other team.

touchdown   A play worth six points, accomplished by gaining legal possession of the ball in the opponent's end zone. It also allows the team a chance for one extra point by kicking the ball or a chance to attempt a two-point conversion.

turnover   The loss of the ball by one team to the other team. This is usually the result of a fumble or an interception.

two-point conversion   A scoring play immediately after a touchdown during which a team can add two points to the score instead of kicking for just one point; in a two-point conversion, the scoring team has one play to run or pass the ball into the end zone from the opponent's 3-yard line in college football and 2-yard line in the NFL.

veteran   A player who has played in the league for several years.

West Coast offense   An offensive philosophy that uses short, high-percentage passes as the core of a ball-control offense.

wide receiver   A player position on offense. He is split wide (usually about 10 yards) from the formation and plays on the line of scrimmage as a split end (X) or one yard off as a flanker (Z).

wild card   The two playoff spots given to the two nondivision winning teams that have the best records in each conference.

wishbone   A formation involving three running backs lined up behind the quarterback in the shape of a Y, similar to the shape of a wishbone.

yard   One yard of linear distance in the direction of one of the two goals. A field is 100 yards. Typically, a team is required to advance at least 10 yards in order to get a new set of downs.

zone defense   A defense in which players who are in pass coverage cover zones of the field, instead of individual players.

BIBLIOGRAPHY

Boston Globe. *Greatness: The Rise of Tom Brady*. Chicago: Triumph Books, 2005.

Boston Herald. *Tom Brady: MVP Most Valuable Patriot*. Champaign, Ill.: Sports Publishing, 2002.

ESPN.com: Tom Brady. Available online at *http://scores.espn. go.com/nfl/players/profile?playerId=2330*.

Hamm, Liza, and Stephen M. Silverman. "Exes Tom Brady, Bridget Moynahan Expecting Child." *People*, February 18, 2007. Available online at *http://www.people.com/people/article/0,,20012266,00.html*.

Official Site of the National Football League: Tom Brady. Available online at *http://www.nfl.com/players/tombrady/profile?id=BRA371156*.

Official Site of the New England Patriots. Available online at *www.patriots.com*.

The Patriots Insider. Available online at *www.PatriotsInsider.com*.

Pierce, Tom. *Moving the Chains: Tom Brady and the Pursuit of Everything*. New York: Farrar, Straus and Giroux, 2006.

Silver, Michael. "Cool Customer." *Sports Illustrated*, April 15, 2002, pp. 34–40.

FURTHER READING

Athlon Sports. *Game Day Michigan Football: The Greatest Games, Players, Coaches and Teams in the Glorious Tradition of Wolverine Football.* Chicago: Triumph Books, 2006.

Boston Globe. *Greatness: The Rise of Tom Brady.* Chicago: Triumph Books, 2005.

Gatto, Kimberly. *Tom Brady: Never-Quit Quarterback.* Berkeley Heights, N.J.: Enslow Publishing, 2005.

Johnson, Pepper, and Bill Gutman. *Won for All: The Inside Story of the New England Patriots' Improbable Run to the Super Bowl.* New York: McGraw-Hill, 2003.

Price, Christopher. *The Blueprint: How the New England Patriots Beat the System to Create the Last Great NFL Superpower.* New York: Thomas Dunne Books, 2007.

Savage, Jeff. *Tom Brady.* Minneapolis, Minn.: Lerner Publications, 2006.

WEB SITES

Official Site of the National Football League: Tom Brady
http://www.nfl.com/players/tombrady/profile?id=BRA371156

Official Site of the New England Patriots—Tom Brady Bio
http://www.patriots.com/team/index.cfm?ac=playerbio&bio=566

The Patriots Insider
www.PatriotsInsider.com

University of Michigan Football
http://www.mgoblue.com/section_display.cfm?section_id=185&top=2&level=2

PICTURE CREDITS

PAGE

9:	AP Images
15:	AP Images
20:	AP Images
26:	AP Images
29:	AP Images
35:	AP Images
39:	AP Images
43:	AP Images
49:	AP Images
55:	© JOHN MOTTERN/AFP/ Getty Images
57:	© MATT CAMPBELL/AFP/ Getty Images
65:	AP Images
69:	AP Images
73:	AP Images
76:	AP Images
81:	© Rick Stewart/Getty Images
87:	© Ezra Shaw/Getty Images
93:	AP Images
99:	AP Images
102:	AP Images
111:	AP Images
118:	© Doug Pensinger/Getty Images
121:	AP Images
125:	AP Images
129:	AP Images

COVER
Getty Images

INDEX

ABOUT THE AUTHOR

RACHEL A. KOESTLER-GRACK has worked with nonfiction books as an editor and writer since 1999. During her career, she has worked extensively with historical topics, ranging from the Middle Ages to the colonial era to the civil rights movement. In addition, she has written numerous biographies on a variety of historical and contemporary figures. Rachel lives with her husband and daughter in New Ulm, Minnesota.